THE FLAVOR SECRET

Using herbs & spices to put flavor back into low-fat, low-calorie, low-cholesterol cooking

Judy Gilliard with Joy Kirkpatrick, R.D.

Library of Congress Cataloging-in-Publication Data

Gilliard, Judy
The Flavor Secret:Using herbs and spices to put flavor back into low-fat, low-calorie, low-cholesterol cooking. / Judy Gilliard with Joy Kirkpatrick, R.D.

Includes index
ISBN 1-56561-037-7 ; $12.95

Edited by: Patricia Richter
Cover Design: Terry Dugan Design
Text Design: Nancy Nies
Editorial Production Manager: Donna Hoel
Art/Production Manager: Claire Lewis
Typesetting/Illustration: Janet Hogge
Printed in the United States of America

Published by
CHRONIMED Publishing, Inc.
P.O. Box 47945

Minneapolis, MN 55447-9727

CREDITS

- Mona Virgilio, nutrition-data breakdown of recipes, editing
- Joy Kirkpatrick, ADA exchanges on all recipes
- Jan Mazza, transcriptions and editing
- Pat Richter, research
- Adam Zack, Jensen's, coordinating ingredients
- Sheila Cluff, Patricia Roberts, and Bruce Good of Royal Cruise Line
- Mark Joseph of the Palms of Palm Springs
- David Wexler, Donna Hoel, and Suzanne Dahl at CHRONIMED
- Milt and Sandra Levinson at Ramon Pharmacy
- Nutritional Data Resources
  Diane Lubich
- Mimi Taylor, Alan Ladd's

RECIPE TESTING

Mona Virgilio, Rose Edgar, Doug Edgar, Joann Frazer, and Jan Izen

Table of Contents

RECIPES

HOW CAN I BEGIN?

In any creative field you can never really remember to thank everyone because there are so many people who contribute. There are the people who lend support when things aren't going according to the script you've written for your life. There are the friends and family who are always there to celebrate the successes. *The Flavor Secret* has been a fun, interesting book to write. Since I changed my style of cooking, over ten years ago, to a more health-conscious style, watching the fat content while keeping the flavor, I have maintained my weight and kept my diabetes under control through diet alone. I have always enjoyed dining out with friends, and I love to entertain at home. I have learned to balance so I don't miss out on anything.

So, here is my list of all the people I have to thank. I got my love of cooking from Aunt Rose, who has been an inspiration to me. She is a great cook and is always willing to try something new. And from Cousin Doug, whom no one can match at the barbecue. Uncle Walt loves growing vegetables and is willing to eat anything we want to test. Cousin Chuck and Jean, from whom I learned a lot about cooking and about testing blood sugars. Aunt Ginny and Uncle Johnny who have taught me about canning the fresh fruits and vegetables they grow. And my biggest fan at the dinner table, my sister, Teri, who can draw anything.

Then there's Mona, who is the assistant everyone dreams of having. She can make sense out of my thoughts, is totally calm, and keeps up with my quick changes. And I need to thank Michele, who, no matter how busy she is, will take time to help when help is needed. And Juanita, who defiantly keeps my home in order. Rose Mary is a great support who sticks by me even in the food halls of Harrods! And Joanne, who happily tested recipes along the way on her family and friends.

My thanks go to Joy who has been my dietitian and partner for 13 years and who always lends support and lets me be crazy. And to Stu and Marlene, who have been like parents, for always being willing tasters.

Finally, thanks to Michael, who keeps everything in working order. To Kent, who keeps me looking great. To Willy, who has the knack of design and keeps me in line. To Kirk, who always has time for a word of support. To Jim, my expert on wine and women. To Dan, who is always there when I call. To Mark Joseph, who lets me talk and share my ideas with the clients of the Palms. To Basil and Larry, for being the best neighbors anyone could ask for. And to David, who will always take the time to brainstorm a new idea.

To you all, my family and friends, thanks. I would have been lost without you.

The Flavor Secret

INTRODUCTION

When I tell people I write cookbooks for the health conscious, they often say, "I don't want to come to dinner at your house!" I assume this is because people equate "health conscious" with food that is neither tasty nor appealing. Well, I want to change your thinking about that and show you how easy it is to cook food that is healthy and that tastes good simply by adding herbs, spices, and extracts. This is *The Flavor Secret.* Using herbs, spices, and extracts, you can enhance the flavor of food while taking out the fat.

Fat is what usually gives food flavor. Fat is also what makes us fat. So, it is fat that we want to eliminate from our diets. When we remove fat from a recipe, however, we need to replace it with something else that is going to add flavor or texture to make the food palatable. But, using too much of anything can be hazardous. For example, no one wants to get a mouthful of oregano or basil (something that can leave you with the impression you've just eaten leaves and twigs). Herbs and spices need to be used subtly, bringing out flavors without overpowering the base food.

When I was writing this book, I focused on the modern, active person who really doesn't have a lot of time to spend in the kitchen. Despite the lack of time, this person still wants to serve top-quality food and promote optimum health. For that reason, I decided to keep most of these recipes simple, illustrating the basic use of herbs and spices. I have included some that are a bit more complex for special occasions, and, believe me, they are worth the extra effort.

When you go through this book, remember that it was designed for efficiency. Sometimes, by spending time at the beginning of the month planning menus, you can save a lot of time in the long run. The same is true with shopping. Make lists for each week in the month and then buy just what you need when you need it. Make your kitchen a place where you want to spend time. A window-sill herb garden can add a wonderful, colorful, and fragrant touch.

For many of the recipes in this book, preparation time is just under 15 minutes. However, some of the cooking times are a bit longer. You might want to read ahead so you can plan your time. All of the recipes allow for some creativity on your part. Perhaps you prefer more or less pepper than the recipe calls for, or you wish to make a dish with more "fire" by adding a touch of cayenne. That's your prerogative. I am trying to give you some good guidelines and stimulate your ideas about how you can change your own favorite recipes to be healthful, fun to cook, and tasty.

I would like to hear from you about the things you like to make. Also, I would like to have some of your favorite family recipes, your mother's or your grandmother's. I'm compiling a book of old family favorites, updated to the healthy lifestyle. I will modify all the recipes I receive to fit this mode and then return them to you. These updated versions will be the basis of a new book. Please send your recipes to me in care of CHRONIMED Publishing, 13911 Ridgedale Drive, Minnetonka, MN 55305.

About Herbs and Spices

The use of herbs and spices almost coincides with man's history. It certainly predates man's written history. It is said that the Chinese were among the first to discover the many uses of herbs and spices, both as medicinals and as flavor enhancers in cooking. Chrysanthemums were originally grown for their medicinal properties and were a valued ingredient in a Taoist elixir. Today in China, chrysanthemums are still used in soups, salads, and teas, besides their use in beautiful floral displays.

A first-century cookbook, attributed to Apicus, a Roman epicurean, features the use of herb combinations as flavor enhancers. One recipe for cooking artichokes includes fresh fennel, cilantro, mint, and rue, pounded together, then reinforced with pepper, lovage, honey, oil, and liquamen (a strong fish-based sauce that Romans used in place of salt).

Spices have been highly prized throughout history, and by the ninth century, they were considered as valuable as gold or silver. Cloves and mace sold for about $18 a pound, and peppercorns were sold by the individual peppercorn.

Around 1699, an Englishman named John Evelyn wrote a book listing 73 salad herbs with details for using each herb. The book's title, *Acetaria: A Discourse of Sallets*, illustrates the traditional classification of herbs. "Sallets" were salad herbs. "Pot herbs" were those cooked in large cooking pots, "sweet herbs" were flavorings, and "simples" were medicinal herb compounds.

Herbs are often coupled with spices, yet there is a difference. Herbs are the leaves of fresh or dried plants. Spices are the aromatic parts—buds, fruits, berries, roots, or bark, usually dried. An example of their relationship is the coriander: the seeds of coriander are used in curries and chili powder. The leaves of the plant are known as cilantro, which is often used in Mexican cooking.

Herbs and spices define specific ethnic flavor preferences. In India, curry is created with as many as ten herbs and spices. In Thailand, curry is used in conjunction with fresh herbs to give a more delicate flavor. The Chinese use their famous five-spice powder along with ginger and garlic to give their food its distinctive quality. In Indonesia, flavor preferences tend to the sweet and sour, and they use lemon grass, tamarind, Kaffir lime, and various chilies. In Europe, herbs are used sparingly with a focus on tarragon and the French *fines herbes*, a combination that includes parsley, chervil, and tarragon, among others. In Greek and Italian cuisine, we find an emphasis on basil, thyme, sage, and oregano. In Mexico, cilantro is combined with various chili peppers and more recently *epazote* leaves to give a kick to refried beans.

In early America, almost every colonial home featured an herb garden, but somewhere along the line we lost sight of the value of herbs in cooking. In 1939, Irma Goodrich Mazza wrote a best-selling cookbook *Herbs for the Kitchen*, which reintroduced the use of fresh herbs to American cooking. Ms. Mazza reminded American cooks what fresh herbs, garlic, and premium olive oils could do to enhance the flavors of traditional American fare. She featured six herbs in her recipes: basil, marjoram, mint, rosemary, sage, and thyme.

During the 1970s and '80s, Americans turned away from the kitchen and headed for fast foods. But now we have entered the 1990s, and we are back to cooking what we eat so we have more control over our health. We want to prepare healthful dishes, but we want to do it without much fuss. Interestingly, the herbs that are the most popular today are the same as Ms. Mazza's six: basil, marjoram, mint, rosemary, sage, and thyme. But we've also added parsley, cilantro, chives, and tarragon to the list.

Today it is easy to have an herb garden. Fresh parsley can be grown in a pot on a windowsill, and mint does very well in the garden. As I describe these herbs and spices in detail, I will give some information on growing them. Check with your local nursery about the specific herbs that will grow well in your area. Remember, a kitchen garden today literally means a garden that will grow inside your kitchen. Have fun with herbs!

The Freshness Test

Fresh herbs are really your best bet, but it's not always possible to get them or grow them. So when you use dried herbs, give them the freshness test by crushing them, using a mortar and pestle. This releases the flavor, enabling you to get the freshest taste out of them when you add them to food. For the most part, you can expect herbs you have grown and dried yourself to last at least two years. Herbs you buy in the store may have been on the shelf for a while already, so test them for freshness when you use them. Herbs from your grocer will usually only remain fresh about a year in your cupboard. When using extracts, make sure you buy ones labeled "pure" rather than "imitation." This is especially important for vanilla.

Harvesting, Drying, and Storing Your Home-Grown Herbs

Some things you'll need to know about caring for herbs, in addition to the tips offered later on growing them, center on how to harvest them. Different parts of the herb are gathered at different times. Obviously if you are growing garlic, the entire plant will be taken at the time you're ready to use it. But annual leafy herbs, such as basil, should be carefully picked, never taking more than ten percent of the growth at a time. The same is true with perennials like sage, thyme, and rosemary. Severe pruning or overstripping of leaves will weaken the plant. Careful pruning or harvesting, on the other hand, results in more vigorous leaf growth, giving you healthier plants.

As a general rule, pick herbs when they contain the highest amount of flavor essence. Leaves should be picked just before the plant is about to flower. Flowers, on the other hand, are picked just before they reach full bloom. Berries and fruits are picked at their peak ripeness. When you are using the above-ground portion of a plant, pick just before the plant begins to flower. Roots, like garlic, or rhizomes, like ginger and turmeric, are collected in the fall, just as the leaves begin to change color.

When storing your herbs, keep in mind that herbal properties may be destroyed by heat, bright light, exposure to air, or the activity of plant enzymes, bacteria, or fungi. So, herbs should be kept in a cool, dry place, with minimum exposure to air and sunlight. This doesn't mean you should hide your collection of kitchen herbs and spices away where you forget to use them. It simply means if you have a choice, put them in the cupboard instead of leaving them on the countertop.

One of the most popular methods of preserving herbs for use during winter months is drying. As a matter of fact, drying actually improves the flavor of some herbs, particularly bay leaves. Bay leaves should be cleaned using a pastry brush, but no water, and then laid out to dry in a warm place on an airy surface, like a screen. They dry in about a week and are ready for storage in air-tight, tinted-glass jars.

Other herbs may be dried in bundles. One easy method is to pinch together a small bunch and secure it with a rubber band or kitchen string. Hang the bunch upside down from a rack in a dry and somewhat cool location. The temperature in the drying area should not exceed 86° F because the essential oils of the herbs will evaporate at this temperature or higher. The kitchen is not really the best place to dry your herbs because of the added humidity from cooking. Try to find a spot that is relatively dry, or at least consistent in humidity.

There is yet another way to dry your herbs. Place fresh herbs in brown paper bags labeled for each herb type. Set the bags in a dry, dark, cool place until the herbs inside are dry and crunchy. Shake them occasionally so they dry evenly. Remove any stems, and prepare them for storage by crushing the leaves or chopping them in your mini-chopper. Always store the dried herbs in airtight jars. Keep the jars away from light to protect the color and flavor of the herbs.

Remember, it doesn't take long for herbs to dry. Never let the leaves become so dry that they disintegrate into powder when they are touched. Usually you can plan to let the herbs dry for a week, then strip the leaves whole from the stems and place them in a jar. Be very careful not to crush them. If there is no condensation in the jar by the next day, the herbs are ready to store.

Using the microwave oven to dry herbs is a quick and effective method. Remove the leaves from the stems after you have given the whole herb a quick rinse to remove any soil or dust. Be sure to pat them dry before you strip the leaves. Then spread the leaves in a single layer between two paper towels. Microwave on high for 2 to 2 1/2 minutes. Store the herbs in airtight, tinted-glass jars.

Freezing is another effective means of storing herbs. Dill, fennel, basil, and parsley can all be frozen for future use. Clean the herbs and put about 2 or 3 tablespoons of each in separate freezer bags. You can freeze them alone, or you can make up bags of your favorite combinations. Be sure to label the bags so you can find the herb you want when you need them. Chopping the leaves and freezing them with a bit of water in ice-cube trays is another freezer-safe method of storing herbs. This is especially nice when you want to use the herbs in sauces and broths. Chop the herbs very fine and fill each cube half with the herbs and half with water. Then freeze.

I like to store my bags of freezer-dried herbs in a plastic freezer-safe box to protect them from freezer burn or other damage and to make them easily accessible when I need them. I put the frozen ice cubes into plastic bags and then place the the bags in plastic freezer-safe boxes. That way the ice-cube trays are available for making ice cubes, and the extra packaging helps to retain the freshness of the herbs. Try to use frozen herbs within about six months.

Of course, storing herbs in vinegars or oils is another method of preserving the taste of summer herbs into the winter months. My recipes for making herbed vinegars are found on page 44.

Basic Herbs, Spices, and Extracts

Here's my suggested list of herbs, spices, and extracts that you might want to have on hand:

ALLSPICE

Allspice is the dried, nearly ripe, berry of the allspice tree, a member of the myrtle family known as *Pimenta officinalis*. The name is derived from its flavor, which is pungent and sharply aromatic, and suggests a mixture of cloves, cinnamon, and nutmeg. Grown in the Caribbean, allspice is also known as pimento, pimenta, Jamaican pepper, or clove pepper. It is used whole or ground in pickling spices, mincemeat, roast meats, and baked goods. Its essential oil is used in meat sauces, catsup, and spice blends for pickles and sausages, as well as for reproducing certain fruit flavors.

The allspice tree is a tropical tree with large, simple leaves and tiny flowers. Today most of the allspice we use comes from Jamaica. Mexico cultivates allspice for export also, but the quality of the fruit is not as good as that grown in the West Indies. Attempts to grow the trees in the East Indies have failed, so allspice remains the one major spice produced exclusively in the Western Hemisphere.

Ground allspice from your local grocer can be kept up to two years. If you use the mortar-and-pestle test, you can assess whether or not your supply is still flavorful. You can also obtain whole allspice berries in one-ounce containers at groceries or from herb dealers. For best results in cooking or baking, use 1/4 to 1 teaspoon of ground allspice for every four servings, or use 3 to 6 whole allspice for the same yield.

ANISE

Anise is an annual herb of the carrot family, cultivated for aniseed, its small, fragrant fruits. It has a licorice-like flavor and is good in baking, in stews, and with vegetables. The extract is also good in espresso in place of liqueur. As a matter of fact, anise is the base of the popular Greek drink, ouzo, and of the French *pastis*. Anise is also known as aniseed, sweet cumin, star anise, Chinese anise, and *illicium*. The plant family from which it comes includes parsley and the magnolia, in addition to the carrot.

In the East, anise is used to flavor duck and pork dishes. In China, it is added to tea and coffee. Today the Chinese star anise, a native of southeastern Asia, has replaced the more expensive aniseed. While it can be grown in North America, anise prefers a high, sheltered, sunny location in a soil with good water retention. The plant is a shrub and can be incorporated into an herb garden in some locations. In the U.S., its cultivation is limited to the Midwest and Eastern states, especially Rhode Island.

In addition to the seeds, both dried and fresh leaves are used to flavor foods, and the fresh leaves especially will give a slightly sweet flavor to fruit and vegetable salads. They are also a tasty addition to shellfish when the leaves are placed in the boiling water in which the shellfish are cooked.

To achieve the best flavor, my "rule of thumb" is to use 1/4 to 1/2 teaspoon of the dried leaves, 1 to 2 teaspoons of chopped fresh leaves, or 4 to 6 whole leaves for a four-serving recipe. It's best to buy or harvest the seeds whole in small quantities because they do not retain their flavor long. Grind seeds just before adding them to the recipe.

BASIL

Basil, or sweet basil, is an annual herb belonging to the mint family. Sweet and pungent, it is an excellent compliment to tomatoes and cucumbers. It enhances the flavor of most cooked vegetables and is also the key ingredient in pesto, the popular sauce for pasta dishes. It is also an ingredient of *fines herbes*, an herbal mixture used in French cooking. It has a minty, mildly peppery taste and a rich, warm aroma.

As a member of the mint family, basil makes a great potted plant in either the kitchen or the garden. It is also known as St. Josephwort, but there are actually fifty or sixty species of basil. The plant usually blooms in August, and the white blooms should be picked off to promote leaf growth. It is the leaves that are used in cooking. The varieties of basil that do well in America are sweet basil, dwarf basil, Italian or curly basil, lemon basil, or purple basil. Because it is a member of the mint family, it is best to contain the plant in a pot, either in a window box, inside your kitchen, or even in the garden. Left unchecked, the plant will spread into the growth plots of other herbs.

While it is commonly available in the dried form from the grocer, dried basil does not compare in taste to that of basil freshly picked from the garden or potted plant. Basil is easy to grow and the fresh leaves can be kept briefly in plastic bags in the refrigerator or frozen with a little water in ice-cube trays.

To use in cooking, for each four servings use 1/8 to 1/4 teaspoon of the dried leaves, 2 to 3 teaspoons chopped fresh leaves, or one small sprig of fresh leaves from the plant.

BAY LEAF

Bay, or sweet laurel, a flavoring agent, is the leaf of the true laurel, a small evergreen tree or shrub native to the Mediterranean. It is cultivated in Greece, Portugal, Spain, and Central America. There is a form of the laurel tree, *Umbellularia californica*, grown in California, which is a much larger tree with leaves used chiefly for their yield of volatile oil. Bay leaves were the laurels used for heroic Greek and Roman wreathes. The term "poet laureate" derives from the use of the bay or laurel leaf in the wreathes used to honor poets.

Whole or ground bay leaf is used to season meats, potatoes, stews, sauces, fish, pickles, and vinegars. However, its dry form is best in cooking. The fresh leaves have a slightly bitter flavor that dissipates if the leaves are left to dry for a few days. Even dried, bay has a strong flavor, and the leaves are sharp, so the leaf itself is discarded after it has flavored the food.

Bay is excellent in soups, stews, and marinades. It is frequently found in French cuisine and imparts a slightly sweet taste. However, it can leave a bitter taste if used too heavily, so I recommend the use of 1 or 2 crushed leaves in servings for four or 1 to 3 whole leaves, but no more. Be sure to remove the leaves before serving the food.

CAPERS

Capers are the unopened flower buds of a deciduous shrub native to the Mediterranean. In Europe, the bush has been cultivated for its flower buds, which are picked, pickled, and sold as a pungent condiment. In our area, it is grown as a greenhouse plant in the northern United States and outdoors in warmer areas.

Today, capers are found commercially packed in vinegar. Used frequently in Mediterranean cuisine, capers add a lot of zest to tomato dishes and eggplant and are especially good with fish. Capers are cured and prepared in salt, then put in a vinegar brine. Their bitter salty taste makes them useful in small quantities.

The Italians place five or six capers on the *antipasto*. In canapes, placing one caper on each instead of sliced olives makes a distinctive change of flavors. For four servings, I use 1 to 2 teaspoons as a garnish or a single tablespoon in sauces.

CARAWAY OR CARAWAY SEED

Caraway is an annual or biennial herb, also from the carrot family. It is cultivated for its small, fragrant fruits, called caraway seeds. However, the fresh leaves and roots from your own herb garden can also be used, and each part of the plant has its own distinctive flavor. Its feathery green leaves resemble the foliage of carrots and taste a bit like the seeds. The root is very sweet and a bit like a parsnip, but much milder in taste. The small, elongated seeds are used in baking, desserts, cakes, and bread. The plants do well in temperate climates and require much the same soil and light conditions as the carrot. Roots and leaves store only briefly in the refrigerator. The seeds last up to two years and should be store in airtight containers and kept away from the light.

Caraway also goes well with meat, potatoes, and cabbage. It is often used in rye bread and with cabbage because it is believed to dispel gas and calm the digestive tract. Add caraway seeds to any dishes that benefit from their unique flavor. In addition to those uses listed above, caraway is often used in soups, stews, cheeses, sauerkraut, and pickling brines. Caraway oil is also used to flavor two digestive-aid liqueurs, Scandinavian *Aquavit* and German *Kummel.*

For four servings, I use approximately 1 to 2 teaspoons of the chopped leaves, and 1 to 2 fresh sprigs only as garnish. If you want to eat the root of the plant, plan one root for each serving. A teaspoonful of the seeds, crushed, really enhances the flavor of baked apples, or add them to boiled potatoes or cabbage. Taste test and use the seeds in quantities that please your taste.

CARDAMOM

A member of the ginger family, cardamom is used in Indian and Middle Eastern-style cooking. Its seeds and oil are used . Ground cardamom seed is used in curries and in pastries, buns, and pies. Its flavor is sweet, aromatic, and pungent. It is also used in espresso and to flavor coffees.

Cardamom pods are the dried fruit of a perennial native to India. Today, we import the seed from Guatemala, Italy, Central America, Mexico, and Ceylon. It does not grow in the North America. Next to saffron and vanilla, cardamom is the third most expensive spice available today.

Cardamom seed can be purchased in the pod or out of the pod as tiny brown seeds, whole or ground. Because the ground or loose seeds lose flavor quickly, it is best to buy whole pods.

Discard the pods themselves before grinding the seeds. Cardamom pods should be green or white, not brown. The brown pods yield a seed that tastes like moth balls, so beware.

The spice may be used much like cinnamon in baked apples, coffee cakes, melon balls, curries, pickles, honey, mulled wine, or grape jelly. Its flavor, which some describe as anise-like, also has a lemony tang. It enhances meats, game, and sausage. Use in small pinches to suit your personal taste. In a fruit salad for four, I use 1/2 teaspoon ground cardamom.

CAYENNE

A member of the nightshade family, the fruit of cayenne, known as African pepper and African chilies, is picked when it has turned red. Then it is left to dry and is ground into a powder. Today, this spice is the ground pod and seeds of various Chili peppers grown in Africa, Mexico, Japan, Nigeria, and the United States.

Cayenne flavors hot, spicy dishes, eggs, and beans. It takes very little cayenne to spice up a sauce or add zest to a chili. This seasoning resists measuring and must be used "to taste." Heat brings out the hotness of cayenne, so when you use it in cooking, add, stir, and taste. Then taste again in five minutes before adding any more.

CELERY SEED

A member of the parsley family, celery seed adds a wonderful flavor to anything in which you'd usually use celery. Its flavor is slightly bitter and it goes well with cheeses, spreads, cocktail juices, and pastry. It is considered a prerequisite in potato salad by some cooks. The seeds add the sweetly aromatic flavor of the fresh celery, plus a slight, natural bitterness of the seed covering, when placed in pastries or used to flavor pot roasts, salad dressings, salads, sauces, soups, stews, and sandwich spreads.

Celery seeds are the dried fruits of the celery plant, a vegetable that is not well suited to home gardens because it requires very rich soil and up to a half year of cool temperatures to mature. Celery seed is available ground in 1 1/4 ounce containers at grocers and whole in 1/2 to 1 1/2 ounce containers. Celery seeds are tiny and brown in color. The whole seed retains its flavor well, but it should be used sparingly because it can be bitter. If you want to maximize the flavor, crush it before using. Celery seasoning tends to become stale quickly, but you can refrigerate it to get better results. It should be kept in an airtight container in a cool, dark place.

For four servings, I use 1/8 to 1/2 teaspoon of the ground seed or 1/4 to 1 teaspoon of the whole seed as flavoring, or 1 teaspoon to 1/2 cup whole seed in pickles.

CHERVIL

Akin to parsley with a slight likeness to tarragon, chervil is one of the four basic *fines herbes* found in the French kitchen. (The others are parsley, chives, and tarragon.) It is an annual herb of the carrot family, native to southeastern Europe and nowadays cultivated in Belgium and California.

It is one of the best herbs for growing in boxes and, if you are lucky enough to have a greenhouse, you can count on having fresh leaf throughout the winter. It can be started from seed in your garden, then transplanted to pots for the winter. A sunny kitchen window can make a wonderful winter greenhouse for many of the herbs in this list, and you can enjoy them fresh throughout the entire year.

The leaves are best used when fresh, but you can refrigerate them in a plastic bag for a while. Although much of the flavor is lost, chervil can be dried and stored in an airtight jar.

Chervil can be used in soups, stews, salads, or in dishes in which you would use parsley. It imparts a mild anise-like flavor, like parsley but more subtle. Always add the leaves at the end of the cooking time to retain the delicate flavor of this herb. My rule of thumb is 1/4 to 1 teaspoon of the dried leaves for four servings. As a garnish, I use 1 to 2 teaspoons chopped fresh leaves or 6 to 8 sprigs for four servings.

CHINESE FIVE-SPICE POWDER

This is an aromatic blend of spices that gives a sweet, pungent flavor to roasted meats and poultry when they are cooked in soy-based sauces. Use it sparingly, however, since overuse can overpower the flavor of the main dish it is used to enhance.

Five-spice powder contains approximately equal portions of finely ground fennel seed, cloves, star anise, cinnamon, and Szechuan pepper. There is also a Chinese eight-spice powder that uses all of the above and ground ginger, aniseed, and licorice. Because it is a blend, it is best to buy this one from the grocer's shelf or from an herb dealer.

CHIVES

The most delicate member of the onion family, chives enhance the flavor of many foods and may be used in stews, stock, sauces, atop sour cream or cheese, added to omelets, or mixed in cottage or cream cheese for spreads or dips.

Chives grow nicely in an herb garden and are often used as the decorative edging plant. They are a perennial and can be started from seed, but starting from the bulbs, or even better, buying the plants already started from the local nursery is your best bet. They do very well in kitchen window-sill gardens during the cold months and flourish outside from spring until fall.

Chives really cannot be dried with any great success, but they may be frozen and stored. However, because the plants are easy and undemanding, it is best to use their leaves fresh. To freeze, cut the stems and fill an ice cube tray half with cut chives and half with water. To dry them, suspend chives individually by their flowered heads from a mesh screen. The fresh floral heads are edible and make a lovely garnish or component in salads.

My rule of thumb is to use 1 teaspoon to 2 tablespoons of the chopped fresh leaves for every four servings, or 6 to 8 whole leaves in herb bouquets. Use 1 tablespoon to each quarter-pound of butter or butter substitute if you want to use chives in herb butters; 2 teaspoons may be added to each cup of dressing in herb salad dressings. Because long cooking destroys their flavor, chives should be added at the last minute.

CINNAMON

Cinnamon is one of the oldest spices known to man. It is used as either the whole bark or in ground form, mainly in baking and pickling. We sprinkle it on toast, add it to cookies, stir it into hot apple cider or cold apple sauce, and find it in candy. Cinnamon is also known scientifically for its antiseptic properties, which explains why it is found in many mouthwashes and toothpastes.

This spice is actually the dried inner bark of trees belonging to several species, all related to the laurel family. The "true" cinnamon tree is native to India and Sri Lanka and is cultivated in various locations in the tropics.

Cinnamon is available from the grocer ground in 1 1/2 ounce to 4 ounce containers, or in quills or sticks in about 1 1/2 ounce containers. The spice usually used in the U.S. is really cassia, the dried ground bark of the trees from the laurel family. It has a stronger flavor than true cinnamon and is a deeper brown, whereas real cinnamon is actually a light yellowish brown. Store cinnamon sticks or ground cinnamon in airtight containers in a cool, dark location.

My rule of thumb for using cinnamon is to add 1/4 to 1 full teaspoon of the ground cinnamon per four servings or 1 small quill or stick per serving. Try cinnamon sprinkled over cooked squash or on peas or spinach. Adding a pinch of chili powder really brings out the flavor. For an unexpected taste, add a pinch of ground cinnamon to a meat stew.

CILANTRO

Cilantro is actually the leaf of the coriander plant, another member of the carrot family. It is one of the most widely used cooking herbs in the world. The leaves are parsley-shaped and have a pungent aroma and taste.

The plant grows well in gardens, preferring dry soil and full sun. Start the plant from seeds in the late spring and expect germination to be slow. The root of the plant can be cooked and eaten as a vegetable, and the seeds, of course, are used as a spice called coriander. By the way, the plant itself has a rather unpleasant odor, so you may want to buy this herb at the grocery. If you do grow it, dry it just as you would parsley, but bear in mind that the dried version is really not comparable to the fresh leaf.

Fresh cilantro does not keep well, however, so try to keep the fresh plant intact and store it in the refrigerator between moistened paper towels, or place the stem ends in a glass filled with water in the refrigerator. Remove any wilted leaves. Don't remove the roots or rinse the herb until you are ready to use it.

Fresh cilantro leaves may be frozen. Chop the leaves finely and place them in ice-cube trays—half cilantro leaves, half water. The seeds, available from the grocer and known as coriander, should be kept in a cool place away from the light in an airtight container.

Cilantro is good with poultry, vegetables, and sauces. It is commonly used in Chinese and Mexican cooking and is also known as Chinese parsley. My rule of thumb for use is almost the same as for parsley, but a little more sparing: one or two sprigs on each plate as garnish or about 3/4 tablespoon of fresh cut leaves for every four servings.

CLOVES

Cloves are actually the dried buds of an evergreen tree of the myrtle family. The tree produces abundant clusters of small red flower buds that are gathered before opening and are then dried to produce the dark-brown, nail-shaped spice we recognize as cloves.

When you step into a spice shop, it is the rich, warm aroma of cloves that usually greets you. Cloves have been used throughout history as a mouth-sweetener. Buy cloves ground in 1 1/4-ounce containers or whole in 1- or 2-ounce containers. Store them in airtight containers in a cool, dark place. Expect them to last on the shelf about a year.

Cloves may be used whole, wrapped in cheesecloth for easy removal after cooking, or ground in drinks, marinades, glazes, breads, and sweets. Ground clove is often used in combination with a bay leaf, or ground cinnamon, ginger, and nutmeg. Cloves have a very strong flavor, however, so it's best to be conservative until you are really comfortable with using the ground form.

Whole cloves are often used to stud a ham and they may be added to the water in which vegetables are boiled or steamed to give a wonderfully warm flavor. Using a whole onion studded with cloves during the last hour of cooking a roast imparts a delicious taste.

For four servings, I use 1/8 to 1/2 teaspoon of ground cloves. In beverages, 1 to 2 whole cloves are best. With roasts or hams, the amount varies for either appearance or taste.

CUMIN

Cumin seed is actually the dried fruit of a small annual herb that belongs to the parsley family. This delicate plant grows in Egypt, western Asia, and the Mediterranean. Often found in Mexican and Indian cooking, cumin was used in Roman times the way we use pepper today.

Ground into a powder, cumin is hot and bitter, and should be used sparingly. For four servings, I use 1/8 to 1/2 teaspoon ground or 1/2 to 2 teaspoons of the whole seed. The seed is minute, yellowish brown in color, and oval shaped, something like a caraway seed. I like using the whole seeds and grinding them with a mortar and pestle just before I use them. Their flavorful oil dissipates rapidly after they are ground. Dry-roasting the seeds before grinding enhances their pungent flavor. Remember, cumin is potent and this spice can dominate the taste if used too generously.

Cumin is used commercially in flavoring liqueurs and cordials. We use it in curries and for pickling. Although ground cumin seed is already a part of chili powder, many Mexican cooks like to add a teaspoon of whole cumin seed per pound of meat in their chili con carne.

Cumin can be grown in your herb garden, but it is fragile. It is an annual that can be started from seed sown in the late spring. It likes sandy soil and warm weather and tolerates most well-drained soils in sunny settings. Because only the seed is usable, however, it is probably more efficient to buy cumin. It is available at the grocer's in 1/2- to 1-ounce containers, ground, or whole in 1 1/2-ounce containers.

CURRY POWDER

Curry powder is actually a blend of ingredients including turmeric, cardamom, coriander, mustard, saffron, allspice, and other spices. It can be used in salad dressings, egg dishes, on poultry, and to make a distinctive savory rice. It is most often associated with the flavors of India.

In the kitchen, you may want to proceed slowly with the use of curry until you are familiar with your blend. You may mix it yourself according to the recipe below, but for your first use, it's really best if it is purchased. Curry may be mild, somewhat hot, or very hot. A small touch of the powder in cranberry sauce to go with roast chicken or a bit in baked fish might be a good way to start.

With my blend, I use about a teaspoon for a mild flavor for each four servings and 2 teaspoons to 1 tablespoon for a spicier flavor. Here's the recipe:

Combine 6 dried red chilies, 2 tablespoons coriander seeds, 1/2 teaspoon mustard seeds, 1 teaspoon black peppercorns, and 1 teaspoon fenugreek seeds in a heavy, cast-iron skillet. Roast over medium heat until dark in color, be very careful not to burn. Leave this to cool, then grind it into a powder with a mortar and pestle. Blend in 1/2 teaspoon ground ginger and 1/2 teaspoon ground turmeric. Curry can be stored up to three months in an airtight jar kept in a cool dark place.

DILL

Dill has long been a favorite flavor in pickles, and it can be found in herb form (dill weed) or as dill seed, used as a spice. A member of the carrot family, it is an easy plant to grow and makes another good addition to an outdoor herb garden. Dill is an annual that tolerates most soils. Sow the seed in the spring, then simply wait for harvest.

Dill is one of the herbs you want to use fresh if at all possible, since the herb loses some of its flavor when dried. It is commercially available ground in 1/2- to 1-ounce containers as seed or as cut leaf. The fresh leaves and stems are available in markets during late summer and early autumn.

Fresh dill leaves can be kept in a plastic bag in the refrigerator for a week or so, or you can freeze them. Chop the leaves finely and mix them with water, then freeze in ice-cube trays. To dry the leaves, hang them in bunches, secured with a twist-tie or rubber band, in a warm, dry, well-ventilated place.

Add dill to whipped nonfat cottage cheese to create a delicious dip for vegetables. It is also very good sprinkled on seafood or meat to achieve a butter-like flavor. Try it with tuna salad and with fresh cucumbers for a refreshing change or in potato salad.

I use 2 teaspoons of chopped dill mixed with fresh vegetables in salads. In cooking chicken, I spread a single dill stem over the poultry before cooking. Two teaspoons of chopped dill with eggs makes a yummy omelet. For four servings, 2 tablespoons of chopped fresh leaves may be used as garnish, or 1 small sprig with leaves as a flavoring in soups and stews.

FENNEL

Fennel is another member of the plant family that includes carrots and parsley. It has a sweet, licorice flavor similar to anise, but a bit milder. Throughout history, fennel was prized for its stems, but today we use it almost exclusively as a seed. I recommend that you try using the leaves.

Fennel can be grown in the garden and is a biennial or perennial, but it can be cultivated as an annual. It may be planted in any soil except clay and the seeds should be sown in the autumn. It has deep green, fern-like leaves something like dill, and the large stems, flattened at the base, look a little like celery. Both the foliage and the stems have a mild licorice flavor.

Keep fresh fennel leaves in a plastic bag in the refrigerator or chop them finely and freeze them with a little water in ice-cube trays. Fennel leaf can also be infused in olive oil or wine vinegar. The dried seeds should be kept in airtight containers in a cool, dark place.

A good addition to pork, fish, or seafood dishes, fennel seed may also be used in stocks, soups, and chowders, as well as rice dishes. My rule of thumb: 1 teaspoon to 2 tablespoons chopped fresh leaves as garnish for four servings; as seed, 1/2 to 1 teaspoon, crushed.

If you decide to try growing some fennel, you can eat the young stems and base raw, just like you would celery.

GARLIC

Used since ancient times, garlic is a perennial herb related to the onion. It is a pungent bulb composed of cloves surrounded by a thin white or purplish sheath. Because seed is rarely produced, garlic is propagated by planting individual cloves. When the green tops ripen and fall over, the bulbs are pulled. Garlic can be stored for several months if kept dry and cool.

Most of the garlic in the United States is grown in California, and much of the crop is dehydrated and sold as garlic powder. If you try it in your garden, you'll want to know that it is a biennial or perennial that prefers rich, light, well-drained soil. Plant individual cloves in the spring—or preferably in autumn—in rich, dry soil, in a sunny spot. Put the bulbs down about 4 inches.

When harvesting garlic, you will be taking the entire plant, so be ready to replant with another bulb or clove. Fresh garlic is at its best at the beginning of the season and generally should be used as it is taken from the garden. If you want to store it, put the garlic in a cool, dry, well-ventilated place away from light. When stored properly, the bulbs should last several months.

Garlic adds a strong, pungent flavor to any dish. It is recognized for its medicinal and curative properties and is used largely in Italian and Mediterranean cooking. It is available in cloves, powdered, and as a salt. Garlic can be added to almost any food. The cloves' papery skins peel easily if you smash them with the flat side of a knife. Many people have objected to the strong odor left by garlic. I use waxed paper on my cutting board and I wash my knives with a little lemon juice to get rid of the smell. The lemon juice also cleans my fingers.

An alternative method for cleaning and using garlic is to plunge the cloves into boiling water for 30 seconds. Drain and then peel them when they are cool. Crush them with the flat edge of a knife, then slice or chop them as required. Of course, using a garlic press is an excellent method for getting all the flavor from a clove. To be sure each batch of garlic contains only the freshly pressed pieces, however, you must thoroughly clean and dry the press after each use. Use a toothbrush to scour the press.

Garlic oil, called an odorless garlic, is now on the market and can be used as flavoring in soups, stews, and pot roasts, but nothing beats the flavor of fresh garlic. For four servings, I use 1/2 to 1 full garlic clove in cooking. When you want just a hint of garlic, rub a crushed clove around the base of a porcelain baking dish or a wooden salad bowl before you add anything else.

GINGER

Ginger is a spice from a perennial plant native to southern Asia.

Found in powdered form or in the produce department as a whole root or rhizome, ginger adds a sharp edge to food. It is used in baking as well as in Oriental cuisine.

Ginger ale and gingerbread both evolved from ginger's use in ancient Greece as a digestive aid. The Greeks ate ginger wrapped in bread after big meals. Today ginger ale is a popular drink known for its stomach-soothing properties. Throughout history ginger has been used for its medicinal properties, and today in China it is considered an important drug.

Ginger is available ground in 1/2-ounce, 1-ounce, and 2-ounce containers at the grocery store. The root, crystallized, dried, and sugared, comes in 8-ounce and 1-pound tins at confectioneries or herb dealers. The root also comes preserved in syrup in jars of varying shapes and sizes. The whole dried root in 1- or 2-ounce containers may be purchased at groceries and markets.

If you buy the fresh root, wrap it in paper towels and seal it in a plastic bag, then refrigerate. It should keep for several weeks. The dried product should be kept in a cool, dark place. Use a sharp knife to prepare your fresh gingerroot for grating. Peel away the rough outer skin only as far as the flesh, then use your ginger grater.

If there is a flavoring that could make a filet mignon taste better, it is ground ginger. Try blending 1/2 teaspoon ginger with salt and pepper, then rub the seasoning mix on both sides of the meat before broiling. Poultry and pot roasts are also delicious when lightly sprinkled with ginger before cooking. Remember, dried ground ginger tastes nothing like fresh and the two are not interchangeable in recipes.

Other dishes in which to include ginger are pies, pickles, puddings, sauces, and baked fruits. My rule of thumb for use in cooking is to add 1/4 to 1 teaspoon ground ginger for each four servings. Use 1 to 4 tablespoons minced preserved ginger as a sauce.

The amount of fresh ginger you use will vary from recipe to recipe, but you should taste-test to determine the amount that suits you best.

LEEKS

Leeks are an annual herb belonging to the lily family. The leek's onion-like flavor is mild and sweet. Leeks look like a very large green onion. They can be somewhat sandy, so they need to be washed well. They can be grown in your garden in a mound of earth surrounded by a trench. The herb develops long stalks underground and broad, flat green leaves above. Leeks are always used fresh.

Leeks add a delicate, light flavor to food and are found frequently in French cooking. They enhance the flavors of meat, fish, and poultry dishes, and may be used as a garnish. Added to pasta, rice dishes, and salads, they impart a slightly oniony taste. I use 1/2 to a whole leek in salads and soups for four. You can serve leeks by themselves as a cooked vegetable.

Leeks make an ideal base for a fresh *bouquet garni. Bouquet garni* is the French term used to describe a bundle of herbs to be used in cooking. The classic combination consists of 3 sprigs of parsley, 1 small sprig of thyme, and 1 small bay leaf, wrapped in an aromatic vegetable wrapping, like the green part of the leek, or a celery stalk. The elements of the bouquet are tied together with string, then added to the soup, stew, or sauce. When the food has cooked, the garni is removed.

There is a dried version of this blend that can be either purchased or mixed up at home. Use equal parts of dried herbs, such as parsley, bay, thyme, or whatever combination you prefer. Place the herbs in a square of cheesecloth and tie the four corners with kitchen string to form a bag. Remove the bag after cooking. Choose herbs suitable for the dish you're cooking.

LEMON PEEL

This is the thin outer peel of the lemon. While fresh is best, lemon peel is available in jars and is good to keep on hand. I've included lemon peel in many of the recipes in this book. It imparts a slightly bitter, citrus flavor and is usually used in small quantities.

MACE

The ground outer coating of the nutmeg seed, mace is used in the same ways as nutmeg. Nutmeg fruits resemble small peaches and when ripe, are quite beautiful inside. The first layer is green, the next layer orange, and the third layer, which becomes the covering that is dried and ground to produce mace, is a brilliant scarlet. When dried, it forms that lacy outer covering over the nutmeg kernel. It takes more than 400 pounds of this covering to make one pound of mace.

Ground mace stores better than almost any other ground spice. Keep it in an airtight jar in a cool, dark place and it quite literally lasts for years and years.

Commonly found in cakes, cookies, pickling, and preserves, mace can also be used in some meat and fish dishes. It blends well with cinnamon, cloves, allspice, and ginger. Its flavor is much stronger than that of nutmeg and in blends, you'll want to use less mace than any other component. When I make a cream sauce or a fish sauce, for example, I use 1/8 to 1/4 teaspoon ground mace and 1/4 teaspoon onion salt with 1/4 teaspoon celery salt. For shellfish, I add a few grains to each serving. The rule of thumb: 1/8 to 1/2 teaspoon ground mace for four servings.

MARJORAM

Marjoram, or sweet marjoram, is a perennial that grows to be about 12 inches tall and has grayish-green leaves and tiny cream-colored flowers. It is native to western Asia and the Mediterranean region, but you can try to grow it in your herb garden. Sow the seed in late spring or early summer (or start the plants indoors and replant outdoors if you live in a colder climate) in medium-rich, finely prepared soil. The plants prefer sunny locations and dryish soil.

Marjoram is the same as oregano; keep it in the refrigerator in sealed plastic bags when fresh, or freeze using the ice-cube tray method.

Similar to oregano, but milder and sweeter, marjoram is very good in sauces, stews, and soups. It is also good over vegetables. Many cookbooks sometimes suggest replacing oregano with marjoram for sweeter, spicier sauces. But the fact is, the oregano on your spice rack might really be marjoram. All marjoram species are also called oregano. While some palates cannot distinguish between the two, there is a difference. When you want oregano flavor, but less of it, use marjoram.

My rule of thumb for four servings is 1/4 to 1/2 teaspoon of crushed dried leaves, 3 or 4 small fresh leaves, if you grow your own, or 1/8 to 1/4 teaspoon of the powdered or pulverized herb.

MINT

Several different flavors of mint can be grown easily in the garden. They grow so well, in fact, that they just might take over. When planting mint in the garden, I recommend planting it in pots and then placing the pots in the soil to contain the growth. You can also plant mint in a bricked-in section of your herb garden as was often done in colonial times. Mint is a perennial but should be replaced about every four years in the garden because it can become woody.

Mint is actually the common name of about 25 perennial species of one family. The common garden mint is spearmint, which has a sweet, strong scent and is widely used in candies, chewing gum, herbal teas, and the like. Applemint, another very common garden mint, has speckled green and white leaves.

Peppermint is often found growing wild in damp locations from Nova Scotia west to Minnesota and south to Florida and Tennessee. Others common varieties include lemon mint, water mint, and round-leaved mint.

Mint is really best when used fresh from the garden. If you want to store it, however, plan to store it only briefly. If you have planted mint in pots in the garden, you can bring the plants into the kitchen in cooler weather and enjoy fresh mint all year long. If you need to dry some, use the hang-dry method and keep the dried leaves in airtight containers in a cool, dry location. You'll lose a lot of flavor with the drying process, so adjust your recipes accordingly.

Mint is one of the most widely used herbs in the world. Chop the leaves and add them to salads and cold drinks. Mint leaves also make a soothing hot tea. Used in cooking, mint enhances the flavors of meat and fish dishes, and mint jelly is often served with roasted lamb. Minced mint leaves mixed with cream cheese make a tasty appetizer. I use 2 tablespoons of freshly chopped mint over baked or broiled fish as a garnish and for flavor. Add 1 or 2 tablespoons fresh mint to boiled carrots, green beans, peas, potatoes, or spinach for a delicious flavor variation. The rule of thumb for dried mint is 1/4 to 1 teaspoon per four servings.

MUSTARD

Mustard is the common name of some annual plants that are grown for their pungent seed and for their leaves, mustard greens. Mustard is native to all of Europe and southwestern Asia and is now cultivated in Austria, England, Germany, Holland, and the western states of the U.S., among others.

Ground mustard or mustard seeds are a wonderful addition to salad dressings, or egg and vegetable dishes. The ancient Greeks and Romans ground up the mustard seeds and spread the powder over their food as a spice. In the seventeenth century, the condiment as we know it today was first produced. Today Dijon, France, supplies over half the world's supply of prepared mustard.

White mustard seeds can be sprouted indoors or in the garden for a crisp and peppery salad herb. Place the seeds on a thin layer of soil in small trays, or even on a piece of damp cloth. Keep them moist and watch them sprout. It takes only about two weeks to get sprouts that are ready to eat (they should be about two inches high). Use these delicate sprouts in salads, on sandwiches, or as a plate garnish. You'll love them.

Store mustard seeds in a cool, dry place, preferably in airtight containers. If you grind the mustard seeds, then add a little water, you'll get a paste that is much like the condiment you buy as prepared mustard, but with a fresher taste.

Use mustard, ground or in seed form, to obtain the same flavor as from the condiment, but more subtly. I use 1/8 to 1 teaspoon of seed for four servings, according to the taste I prefer. When I cook mustard greens, I find a pound to a pound-and-a-half is sufficient for four. When using prepared mustard, I taste test.

NUTMEG

Nutmeg is the seed of the nutmeg tree native to the Moluccas, or Spice Islands, of Indonesia. The dried coating over the center kernel of the nutmeg, which is the pit of a yellow, apricot-like fruit, is known as mace.

Nutmeg has a wild, nutty, and distinctive flavor that is very fragrant. It is very good in desserts and for baking and can be purchased as a ground powder or you can buy it whole and grind it with a special nutmeg grinder or grater. Early spice merchants often carried nutmeg in a special container with a grater attached so the spice could be ground fresh when needed.

Nutmeg goes well with rich foods. It is used in many filled pastas in Italian cuisine, mixed into the stuffing or ground on the top at the last minute. Nutmeg is known to particularly complement milk and cheese dishes. I like to use it with vegetables. Cabbage, kale, cauliflower, spinach, and sweet potatoes all benefit from the flavor-enhancing quality of nutmeg. I also like to sprinkle each serving of fruit salad with a few grains of ground nutmeg and a tablespoon of vanilla yogurt. For four servings, I use 1/8 to 1 teaspoon of ground nutmeg or a few grains of freshly grated whole nutmeg.

Incidentally, nutmeg is known medicinally as an aid to digestion, so it often appears in desserts served at the end of a meal.

ORANGE PEEL

The outer skin of the orange, orange peel is best when used fresh. Keeping a jar of dried on hand, however, is helpful for those times when you want to be creative in the kitchen, but you don't have the fresh fruit available. Orange peel is a little less bitter than lemon peel. It's available from your local grocery store in 1 1/2 ounce jars and can be kept on the shelf for about a year.

OREGANO

Oregano is really a form of wild marjoram and a member of the mint family. It can be started from seed and grown in the herb garden as a perennial. Sow in late spring on a warm site where the soil is nutrient rich and dry. Oregano has beautiful miniature lavender flowers and grows into a leafy bush about 2 1/2 to 3 feet tall.

You can store the fresh leaves in a plastic bag in the refrigerator, or you can freeze them using the ice-cube tray method previously mentioned. If you want to dry the leaves, tie the stems together or secure them with a rubber band and hang them in a dry, well-ventilated place for a week or two. You'll know they're ready to be put into jars if the leaves crumble. (See the earlier section on drying herbs for more information.)

Oregano has a somewhat stronger flavor than marjoram, but its flavor varies depending on soil and climate and it is somewhat stronger than that of marjoram. Use oregano when you want a zesty taste. Use marjoram when you want a milder, more subtle flavor. Italian and Mexican cooking make full use of oregano. As a matter of fact, the word "oregano" is Spanish for marjoram.

Oregano is also known as "Mexican sage" because of its wide use in Mexican cuisine.

The dominant herb in most Italian pasta sauces, oregano is excellent when used with tomatoes, peppers, zucchini, eggplant, and in dips. I like to add about 1/2 teaspoon of dried oregano to vary my potato salad, and 1/2 teaspoon of the dried herb is about right for plain tomato sauce. Use a full teaspoon of minced fresh oregano when it's available from the garden.

PAPRIKA

Paprika is a mild, ground, reddish pepper that is good with chicken, eggs, and dressings, and also makes a nice garnish to add color to any light-colored dish. Poultry, shellfish, salads, rice, fish, scrambled eggs, macaroni, mashed potatoes, appetizers, soups, and gravies all may be flavored and garnished with paprika.

I recommend that you buy the best quality of paprika you can find, but be careful, some of it can be extremely spicy. If the container describes it as "Spanish" paprika, for example, it's really more like cayenne. Keep paprika in an airtight container in a dark, cool location in your kitchen. It loses its flavor and aroma quickly and becomes brown in color and stale to the taste if kept too long.

For four servings, I recommend 2 teaspoons for mild flavoring and a tablespoon or two for more pungent taste. As a garnish, vary amounts according to the appearance of the dish. By the way, paprika was found to contain more vitamin C than any citrus fruit, so you'll be glad to know it adds more than just color to your food.

PARSLEY

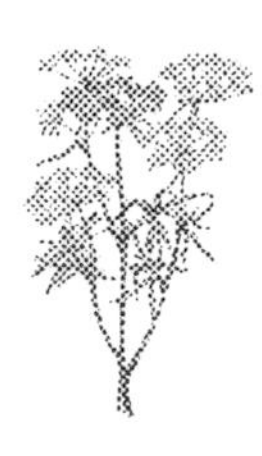

Parsley is a biennial herb of the carrot family that comes in more than 30 varieties. It is easy to grow indoors in a pot or outdoors in the herb garden. Plant the seeds anytime from early spring to early summer. Germination is slow but can be speeded up by watering the freshly planted seeds, which are drilled down into the earth about 3 inches, with boiling water. Parsley plants like rich, moist, open soil and either partial shade (in the warmer regions of the country) or full sun (in the cooler areas).

Store fresh parsley leaves in a plastic bag in the refrigerator or sprinkle them with water and wrap them in paper towels. Even better, cut the fresh stems and place them in a glass of cold water. Keep the glass in the refrigerator for up to a week. If you want to dry them, use the hanging method and keep them in an airtight container away from light and dampness.

Parsley is probably the best known of the leafy herbs. It is always best when used fresh, but it is available commercially dried. Parsley has a light, herbal flavor that is very good in soups, stews, sauces, and salad dressings. Sprigs of parsley as a garnish add color and eye appeal to any dish. Parsley is a rich source of vitamins A and C, and when eaten after a meal, it is an effective breath freshener.

Use parsley in cheeses, eggs, fish, meats, poultry, salads, sauces, and vegetables—in short with almost anything. My rule of thumb for using fresh parsley as a garnish is one or two sprigs per person. In cooking, use a teaspoon or two of the dried leaves for four servings. A tablespoon of chopped fresh leaves in servings for four adds flavor and color.

PEPPER

A spicy berry, pepper comes in three familiar forms: black, green, and white. Having three pepper mills—one for each kind of pepper—is a good idea for quick use in your cooking and for your table.

Pepper is actually the dried fruit of a vine, *Piper nigrum*, that is native to the East Indies and is cultivated in Indonesia, Malaysia, India, Brazil, Madagascar, and Sri Lanka. Because its use is so varied and universal, pepper is known as the king of spices.

Pepper is, of course, available ground, but buying the whole peppercorns in 1 1/4 -or 2-ounce, 4-ounce, or even larger containers and grinding the pepper at the time you need it is really the best. Pepper kept as peppercorns retains its freshness much longer and can be kept almost indefinitely. Keep peppercorns in airtight containers away from light and moisture, preferably in a cool place.

While the best way to use pepper is still to give the mill a few turns just before serving, there are some variations of the uses according to the color of the pepper. Green peppercorns can be mixed into mayonnaise for seafood or egg salads, or add them to cream-based sauces with veal or duck. Black pepper is the traditional form for almost any dish. Use white pepper when you want the flavor of pepper but you don't want the black specks, such as in white sauces, egg dishes, or with mayonnaise.

Pepper will enliven almost any dish you prepare. For black pepper, use 1/8 to 1/4 teaspoon of ground black pepper or 4 to 12 whole peppercorns in servings for four. Ground white pepper should be added in 1/4- to 1/2-teaspoon measures to four servings or use 4 to 12 whole white peppercorns. To garnish, a few turns of the peppermill should be just right.

Of course, there is also red pepper. This variety comes crushed as pods or whole seeds in 1 1/4-ounce bottles from the grocer. It is available ground also. Use this form sparingly since it is the hot one. I use 1/16 to 1/8 of a teaspoon of crushed red pepper for four servings. Or, 1/8 to 1/4 teaspoon of the ground version.

POPPY SEEDS

These are tiny black, or slate-colored seeds with a sweetish, nutty taste that is good in baking. Interestingly, the poppy seeds we use in baking are those of the opium poppy native to the Middle East. The plant is very attractive and has pink, white, or lilac-colored flowers. The spice is the ripe seed. The spice, of course, has no narcotic properties. The medicinal derivatives—opium, morphine, heroin, and codeine—come from alkaloids in the sap of the unripe seed pods.

It is illegal to grow the opium poppy in the United States. Poppy seeds are available whole in 1/2 -to 1 1/2-ounce containers from herb dealers or grocers. The seeds should be stored in a cool, dark place and may be expected to last on the shelf for about 2 years.

Poppy-seed breads and rolls are tasty and attractive, and poppy seeds can be used to make a delicious dressing for fruit salad. They are good used in eggs, rice, and pasta dishes, on vegetables, and in salads. For four servings, I use approximately 1 tablespoon of seed for flavoring or 1/2 to 1 full cup of seed for cake fillings.

ROSEMARY

Rosemary is a fragrant, strongly flavored leaf that looks like a miniature pine needle. It is very good with chicken and Cornish game hens and was used in ancient times to preserve meat. It is excellent when used fresh and can be easily grown in the herb garden. But remember, it's an evergreen shrub and you may not want something so permanent in the garden.

Rosemary is a woody, pine-scented, evergreen that grows to 3 feet in height in most parts of the U.S. In California, creeping rosemary is widely used as a groundcover and cascade over garden walls. Its misty blue color is reminiscent of antique porcelain. Rosemary is found in profusion in the moist climates of North Carolina and Virginia, where it was first planted as a border plant by early colonists. It is ideal to grow in your kitchen in a pot for use when you need it. Outdoors, it requires well-drained soil and a warm, wind-sheltered location. New plants can be started from cuttings or seed. Flowers appear in late spring to early summer.

To store fresh sprigs, place them in a plastic bag in the refrigerator and they should last for several days. Even better, place cut stems in a glass of cold water, then keep this little bouquet in the refrigerator for a few days. Dried rosemary has just as interesting a flavor as the fresh leaves and its use is extensive. You can dry the leaves using the hanging method, but be sure you strip the leaves off the stems before storing them in an airtight container in a dark, cool place.

Place a fresh rosemary leaf in each fruit cup before serving, or blend in a teaspoon of minced fresh rosemary when beating eggs for scrambling. Rosemary is good with fish, game, meat, poultry, and in soups. My rule of thumb is to use about 1/4 to 1 teaspoon of the dried leaves or 1/2 to 2 teaspoons of the fresh, chopped leaves for every four servings..

SAFFRON

This is the most expensive spice available, and its yellow-gold color seems fitting since it is "worth its weight in gold." At nearly $500 an ounce, you'll want to use it sparingly. Saffron is made from the stigmas of the flower *Crocus sativus*, a member of the iris family, native to southern Europe and Asia. It takes about 250,000 flowers to yield one pound of saffron, so you won't find this in an herb garden. Luckily, you only need a tiny bit in most dishes. Don't be concerned about saffron's red color when you buy it in dried form. It will still impart a yellow-gold color when added to food.

Commercially, saffron comes in threads (the actual flower stigma) or as a powder. The powder is usually sold in 1/4-ounce quantities, and the threads are usually bottled in 1-ounce containers. Buy only a little at a time because saffron loses its flavor very quickly. Store it in airtight containers away from light.

Saffron is a traditional addition to many Spanish, Indian, and Mediterranean dishes, and may be used in meat, fish, poultry, rice, and pasta dishes. Used sparingly, saffron has a pleasant taste and is richly aromatic. Used heavily, it is bitter. If you want to use saffron to color a rice dish, for example, soak the threads before you use them, for a more uniform coloring. For four servings, I use about 2 to 4 threads in a sauce that serves four, or 2 to 4 threads in baking (each thread is about 1-inch long).

SAGE

There are over 700 species of plants that have become known as sage. They are known generically as salvia and are all members of the mint family. The one we savor in the kitchen is native to the North Mediterranean coast. This variety prefers limestone soil and full sunny slopes. If you want to grow sage, check with your local nursery. Some varieties of sage can be grown in home gardens, both for the herb value and as an ornamental.

Not all sage that can be grown in the U.S. is of equal culinary quality. The sage considered to have the best flavor grows wild on the rocky hills of what was Yugoslavia and Serbia, and is known as dalmatian sage. It has an aromatic fragrance and a slightly bitter taste.

Fresh sage, either home grown or from the grocer, can be kept in the refrigerator. When sealed in plastic bags, it will remain fresh for a few days. Dried sage leaves should be kept in airtight containers in a cool, dark place. Sage leaves are grayish-green; once past their prime, the color becomes dull, fading to almost totally gray. Normally, you can plan to keep sage about a year, if you purchased it, and about two years if you've grown it and dried it yourself.

There are so many uses of this herb that consumption in the U.S. alone tops 1.5 million pounds a year. Of course, we probably all think of Thanksgiving Day turkey dressing when we think of sage, but sage enhances the flavors of cheese, fish, game, meats, poultry, salads, and vegetables.

To use sage, mince fresh, tender young leaves and tips and use them much as you would parsley or chives. I recommend adding 1/2 teaspoon of dried sage for four servings. With chopped fresh leaves, use 1 teaspoon for four servings.

SAVORY

Savory is also a member of the mint family and it comes in two common varieties: summer and winter. Winter savory has the same properties and uses as summer savory, but it is an evergreen and a much hardier plant. Summer savory is an attractive, slender, fragrant annual with tiny tubular, pale-pink and lilac-colored flowers. It prefers a sunny spot and will grow to about 17 inches tall.

You can buy dried savory in the grocery in 1/2 -to 1-ounce containers. Store dried savory in airtight containers, away from light. If you decide to grow your own, store the fresh leaves in a plastic bag in the refrigerator, or chop the leaves finely and freeze them in ice-cube trays, using half herb and half water in the mix. Remove the cubes from the trays, place them in plastic bags, then store the filled bags in a freezer-safe container. If you decide to dry your own leaves, hang them in a dark, warm, well-ventilated place.

In general, savory has a thyme-like taste that is good with meats and fish. It is often used in sausages, stuffings, soups, and bean dishes. Summer savory has a pleasant piquant flavor, while the winter variety, which is a bit more coarse, has a stronger taste.

Use dried savory on meat, poultry, and vegetable dishes. Use fresh savory with fish, eggs, and in salads and stuffings. For four servings, I use 1/2 to 1 teaspoon of dried leaves, or 1 teaspoon to 1 tablespoon of chopped fresh leaves. Fresh, this herb also makes an attractive garnish to any plate.

SESAME SEED

Sesame seed is the dried fruit of a tropical annual herb that grows in Asia and the southwestern United States. Today, it is principally supplied to the world from India. The plant is cultivated for both its seeds and for sesame oil, which can be used in cooking much the same as olive oil. Sesame seeds are used to make the oil, which comes in either a light or a dark variety. The dark oil adds an Oriental flavor to cooking.

Sesame seed can be purchased from your local grocery in 1- to 1 1/2-ounce containers. Store it in an airtight container away from light, in a cool location.

Sesame has a mild nut-like flavor that is excellent when toasted. It is also delicious when used on rolls and in breads. Sesame seed can be used in soups, salads, salad dressings, vegetable dishes, rice, and pasta, as well as in baking. In Asian countries, the macerated seeds are made into a paste and spread on bread much as we might spread butter (if we were to be eating butter these days). Also many tons of sesame seed are used annually in the manufacture of the rich candy, halvah. In Mexico, the popular mole sauce is also made from a mixture of chili peppers and sesame seeds.

My recommendation for cooking with sesame seeds is to use 1 teaspoon for four servings or up to 2 tablespoons of whole seeds, depending on the recipe.

TARRAGON

Tarragon is a perennial herb that can be grown in a pot, but is a bit fussy about conditions. It is principally grown in Southern Europe and the culinary variety preferred is the French tarragon. Russian tarragon, another variety, is considered to be much more coarse. French tarragon or *Artemisian dracunculus* will not grow from seeds; plants must be started by propagating stem cuttings or dividing the roots of an established plant.

If you try to grow French tarragon in a pot, remember that it does not tolerate overwatering and prefers the soil to be dry. In the garden, it is likewise a bit demanding; you may have to add some rich peat to the soil to help the plants flourish. Russian tarragon, on the other hand, often does well in the garden, but where French tarragon has a delicate anise-like flavor, Russian tarragon has a slightly bitter and more pungent taste.

To store the fresh leaves, place them in a plastic bag and keep them in the refrigerator for a few days. Fresh leaves can also be frozen in ice cube trays, or try preserving them in white-wine vinegar. Of course, wine vinegar with tarragon is a classic, but preserving tarragon leaves in vinegar is a delicious way of keeping fresh leaves on hand for future use. The tarragon in vinegar should be packed and sealed in sterilized jars. Tarragon can also be preserved in oil using this same technique.

Dried leaves are available commercially in 1- and 1 1/2-ounce containers. Dried tarragon should be kept in a cool, preferably dark place, in airtight jars. Remember, however, that dried tarragon loses its flavor very quickly and when it is too old to use, it tastes a bit like hay. You can dry fresh tarragon in a warm, well-ventilated place. Before storing, strip the leaves from the stems.

French tarragon's rich, sweet taste is a mainstay of French cuisine. It is the main seasoning in *bearnaise* sauce, and a key component of the traditional French *fines herbes.* (You can create your own fines herbs by combining tarragon, chives, chervil, and parsley.) Tarragon is good in vegetables, meat, and all fish and shellfish. I especially like to use it to flavor chicken dishes. For four servings, I use approximately 1/4 to 1/2 teaspoon of dried tarragon or 1/2 to 2 teaspoons of the chopped fresh leaves. When I have whole leaves, I put in 1 to 4 for four servings.

THYME

Another member of the versatile mint family, thyme is native to the Mediterranean regions and to Asia Minor. There are actually about 400 species of the genus Thymus. French thyme (also called German or English thyme) is a perennial herb whose leaves provide the common thyme of the spice shelf. Native to Southern Europe, French thyme today is cultivated in France, Spain, and the United States.

Thyme grows easily in a garden or planted in a pot by the kitchen window. Start the plant from seed in the early summer, by dividing plants in the spring, or from cuttings from mid-spring to early summer. Thyme prefers dry soil and full sun. Harvest the stems just before the plant flowers, generally from late summer to early autumn.

You can store fresh thyme leaves in plastic bags in the refrigerator, or strip the leaves off the stems and store them in ice-cube trays in the freezer. Dried leaves are available commercially in 1/2-to 1 1/2-ounce containers and should be stored in airtight containers in a cool location, away from light. To dry thyme from your garden, secure bunches together with string or rubber bands, and hang in a warm, dry, well-aired location. I recommend stripping the dried leaves from the stems before putting them into storage containers.

Thyme has a distinctive, pleasant flavor that is very good with poultry, meat, seafood, tomato-based sauces, and in salad dressings. Interestingly, thyme was used in ancient times as a meat preservative and later was introduced into cooking. Thyme is very pungent when fresh, however, so it must be used sparingly. It is one of the ingredients of the *bouquet garni*, or herb bundle, that is used to season meats, soups, sauces, and vegetables. It is especially appropriate in any dish that is cooked slowly, such as stews, soups, or sauces.

For four servings, I recommend using about 1/8 to 1 teaspoon of the dried leaves, as indicated in the recipe, or 1 to 2 teaspoons of freshly minced leaves. You can also grind the leaves, but remember the grinding will concentrate the flavor so use only 1/8 to 1/2 teaspoon of ground thyme.

TURMERIC

This perennial herb is a member of the ginger family native to Southern Asia. It has been cultivated since ancient times in China and Indonesia and is today grown in India, Jamaica, and Peru. Tumeric is a rhizome, which means it has no seeds. The roots produce a large usable tuber, something like a bulb, from which new plants grow.

Generally, you will find turmeric, ground, in 1/2- and 1 1/4-ounce containers at the grocer. You can also buy the root from herb dealers and grind the turmeric yourself, if you prefer. Store ground turmeric in airtight jars in a cool location away from light.

A ground, brilliant yellow spice with a peppery aroma and a ginger-like flavor, turmeric adds the golden color to curry powder. It is related to ginger, as a matter of fact, and has been a mainstay in Indian curries for thousands of years. Tumeric is still used as a dye for cloth in China. Its culinary use is generally reserved for sauces and stuffings, savory rice dishes, egg dishes, or on fish. Add a small amount of turmeric blended with dry mustard to French dressing for a new flavor and appearance.

Turmeric is sweet enough to be an alternative to saffron in baking and it gives a rich color and flavor to rice dishes. I use 1/8 to 1 teaspoon for four servings when I use the ground form. In curry blends that yield a total of about 16 ounces, I use 4 ounces of ground turmeric. You'll want to taste test your own curry blends, however, to achieve a spiciness that agrees with your palate.

Extracts

Liquid extracts are one of the newest forms of preserved herbs and spices. The essential oils of the herbs and spices are combined with alcohol and water to form a concentrated seasoning. Extracts may be added to foods at the last moment before serving. Since extracts are highly concentrated, they should be added drop by drop until you achieve the exact flavor you want.

Extracts can add a lot of flavor by bringing out a flavor or adding flavor to even the most basic dish. Try adding different extracts to coffee, for example, to make flavored coffees without adding alcohol. Extracts can be stored at room temperature and will keep over an extended period if they are carefully and tightly covered after each use. Naturally, some evaporation will occur over time because of the alcohol base used in extracts.

Remember, extracts can be overpowering because they are highly concentrated, so use them sparingly at first. I recommend using 5 to 10 drops in servings for four, but personal taste will govern your use. Whenever possible, use pure extracts rather than "imitation", especially vanilla.

Here is a list of the most common extracts to keep on hand.

- Almond
- Anise
- Beef
- Brandy
- Chicken
- Lemon
- Orange
- Rum
- Vanilla

HERB BLENDS

Herb blends can be customized to your individual taste. The blends listed here are all made with dried herbs and should be mixed in a mini-chopper. Herb blends make nice gifts if you put them in small containers. My friend Joanne used baby food jars topped with a colorful fabric and tied with ribbon. This gift was a big hit with all her children's teachers. A small jar of your own personal herb blend, coming directly from the warmth of your kitchen to a lucky friend, is an environmentally friendly and useable gift, sure to please.

For these herb mixes, I used "parts" so you can create whatever size batch you need. For your own kitchen, I suggest you use 1 tablespoon as the "part." If you are blending herbs to use for gifts, you might want to use a cup or a half cup, depending on how much of the blend you want to give away.

Herb Salt

2 parts onion powder
1 part garlic powder
1 part dry parsley
1 part marjoram
1 part light salt
1/2 part basil

Greek Blend

2 parts garlic powder
1 part lemon peel
1 part oregano
1/2 part ground black pepper

Italian Blend

2 parts basil
2 parts marjoram
1 part garlic powder
1 part oregano
1/2 part thyme
1/2 part rosemary
1/2 part crushed red pepper

Mexican Blend

1 1/2 parts cumin
1 part onion powder
1 part garlic powder
1/2 part ground ginger
1/2 part paprika
1/2 part oregano
1/2 part dry mustard
1/4 part cayenne pepper
1/2 part parsley flakes

Vegetable Blend

1 part marjoram
1 part basil
1 part chervil
1/2 part tarragon
1/2 part celery seed

Chicken Blend

2 parts marjoram
1 part basil
1 part parsley
1 part dill weed
1 part paprika

Dip Blend

4 parts dill weed
1 part garlic powder
1 part chervil

Basic Herb Blend

4 parts parsley
2 parts chopped chives
2 parts dill weed
2 parts oregano
1 part rosemary
1 part thyme

Herb-Flavored Vinegars

Herbed vinegars make wonderful gifts. You can use one herb or groups of different herbs together to create different flavors and appearances. You must use fresh herbs for this, however. My favorite herbed vinegars are basil, tarragon, and dill.

For each of these recipes, use

1 cup of lightly bruised herbs (rolled in your hand to bruise)

2 cups rice-, red-, or white-wine vinegar

1. Pour boiling water in a jar that you can seal; sterilize the jar then pour the water out.

2. Put the herbs in the jar.

3. In a saucepan, bring the vinegar to boil.

4. Pour vinegar over herbs and seal. Let stand for two weeks, shaking the bottle occasionally.

5. In a clean bottle rinsed with very hot water, pour the vinegar through cheese cloth or a coffee filter. Place a sprig of the fresh herb in the bottle to make an attractive presentation.

To make a garlic or shallot-flavored vinegar, use the same method, but use 1/4 cup chopped garlic or shallots.

To go the opposite direction and preserve your garden-fresh tarragon for later use, use the same method but increase the amount of tarragon to 2 cups and decrease the amount of vinegar to 1 cup.

My Favorite Herbs Chart

Here's a list of foods and their herbal flavor enhancers. Compiled some time ago, this chart represents years of kitchen testing and lets me reference quickly what herbs I like to use with various foods. I keep the chart posted in my kitchen and when I'm being creative, I consult it to get the best out of whatever I am cooking.

Dressings

cream—tarragon
French—tarragon
Russian—tarragon
salad—basil, dill, marjoram, tarragon
sour cream—chive, dill

Eggs

basil, chives, marjoram, oregano, tarragon, thyme

Fish

baked—basil, cloves, sage, tarragon, thyme
boiled—bay, fennel
broiled—basil, marjoram, oregano
lobster—tarragon
salt—sage, thyme
shrimp—basil

Fruit

cinnamon, cloves, mint, rosemary

Meat

beef—basil, rosemary, savory
ham—cloves, mustard, tarragon
hamburger, meatballs—basil
lamb—garlic, mint, oregano, rosemary
liver—basil
pork—cayenne, chili, cinnamon, cloves, rosemary, sage, thyme
pot roast—bay, thyme
sausage—marjoram, sage, savory
stew—basil, cinnamon, marjoram, oregano, thyme
veal—basil, curry, oregano, rosemary, sage, thyme

Poultry

chicken—marjoram, sage, tarragon
fricassee—basil, cinnamon, rosemary, thyme

Potatoes, Pasta, Rice

potatoes—basil, caraway, chives, marjoram, savory
pasta—basil, oregano
rice—fennel, saffron
sauces—sage

Salads

chicken—chive, oregano, tarragon
egg—marjoram, tarragon
fish—chive, marjoram, oregano, tarragon
green—basil, chive, marjoram, mint, tarragon, thyme
vegetable—oregano

Sauces

general—parsley
butter—basil, chives, marjoram, tarragon
cheese—chives
tomato—basil, oregano, sage, thyme
white—basil, curry, marjoram, tarragon

Soups

chicken—bay, marjoram, sage, thyme
clear—basil
cream—chive, rosemary, sage, tarragon
fish—saffron, tarragon
lentil, pea—basil, oregano, rosemary, savory, thyme
mushroom—tarragon
potato—chives, curry
tomato—basil, sage
vegetable—basil, bay, marjoram

Vegetables

general—basil, parsley
beans—basil, cloves, marjoram, sage, savory
broccoli—caraway, oregano
Brussels sprouts—marjoram, sage
cabbage—caraway, mint, tarragon
carrots—basil, bay, marjoram, mint, oregano, thyme
cauliflower—marjoram, nutmeg
lima beans—sage, savory
mushrooms—marjoram, oregano, tarragon, thyme
onions—basil, oregano, thyme
peas—basil, marjoram, mint, oregano, sage, tarragon, thyme
spinach—marjoram, nutmeg, rosemary
squash—cinnamon, cloves, thyme
tomatoes—basil, bay, clove, marjoram, nutmeg, oregano

FINAL WORD ON HERBS

Before we leave the discussion of herbs and their uses, it is important that you recognize one thing more. Herbs not only impart flavor and allow creativity in your cooking, they also allow creativity in your gardening. They have traditionally been a very decorative part of both formal and informal gardens. If you are interested in laying out an herb garden, you should consult your local garden club or visit some of the colonial villages to see the many interesting geometric patterns in which herb gardens were grown. Growing your own herbs can be both pleasing to the eye and a year-round pleasure to the palate.

HERB SPREADS AND APPETIZERS

Cheddar Cheese Spread

7 1/2 oz. dry-curd cottage (or hoop) cheese
3 oz. shredded cheddar cheese
2 Tbsp. sun-dried tomatoes
1 tsp. basil

1. Put all ingredients in food processor and process with steel blade until smooth.
2. Put spread in air-tight container and refrigerate.

Serves 6.

Nutrient information per serving:

calories - 80; protein - 8 gm.; carbohydrate - 1 gm.; fat - 5 gm.; saturated fat - 3 gm.; pecentage of calories from fat - 54; sodium - 92 mg.; cholesterol - 17 mg.; fiber - 0 gm.

ADA exchange value: 1 medium-fat meat

Cream Cheese Spread

This is a good basic spread to have on hand to serve with fat-free crackers or to fill celery sticks.

8-oz. pkg. fat-free cream cheese
1/2 tsp. celery seed
1/4 tsp. dill weed
1/4 tsp. thyme
1/4 tsp. marjoram
2 tsp. parsley

1. Place all ingredients in food processor with a steel blade and pulse until well blended.
2. Put the mixture in an air-tight container and refrigerate.

Serves 6.

Nutrient information per serving:

calories - 33; protein - 5 gm.; carbohydrate - 1 gm.; fat - 0 gm.; saturated fat - 0 gm.; percentage of calories from fat - 0; sodium - 227 mg.; cholesterol - 7 mg.; fiber - 0 gm.

ADA exchange value: 1 lean meat

Cheddar Olive Spread

7 1/2-oz. dry curd cottage cheese (or hoop cheese)
3 oz. shredded cheddar cheese
4 Spanish olives (stuffed with pimentos)
1/4 tsp. chervil
1/8 tsp. crushed red pepper

1. Put cheese in food processor and process with steel blade until smooth.
2. Drop olives in processor while it is running. Process until olives are just chopped.
3. Place in an air-tight container and refrigerate.

Serves 6.

Nutrient information per serving:

calories - 81; protein - 8 gm.; carbohydrate - 1 gm.; fat - 5 gm.; saturated fat - 3 gm.; percentage of calories from fat - 57; sodium - 154 mg.; cholesterol - 17 gm.; fiber - 0 gm.

ADA exchange value: 1 medium-fat meat

Feta Cheese Spread

7 1/2 oz. dry curd cottage cheese (or hoop cheese)
4 oz. Feta cheese
1 tsp. Greek seasoning blend (see page 43)

1. Place all ingredients in food processor and process with steel blade until smooth.
2. Spoon into an air-tight container and refrigerate for at least one hour before serving.

Serves 6.

Nutrient information per serving:

calories - 71; protein - 7 gm.; carbohydrate - 1 gm.; fat - 4 gm.; saturated fat - 3 gm.; percentage of calories from fat - 52; sodium - 214 mg.; cholesterol - 18 mg.; fiber - 0 gm.

ADA exchange value: 1 medium-fat meat

Goat Cheese Spread

Goat cheese has become one of the favorites of the '90s. Here is a way to take 75 percent of the fat out while keeping all the wonderful flavor.

4 oz. goat cheese
8 oz. nonfat cream cheese
1 tsp. vegetable herb blend (see page 43)

1. Mix all ingredients in food processor with steel blade.
2. Place in an air-tight container and refrigerate.

Serves 6 (2-oz. servings).

Nutrient information per serving:

calories - 83; protein - 8 gm.; carbohydrate - 2 gm.; fat - 4 gm.; saturated fat - 3 gm.; percentage of calories from fat - 43; sodium - 438 mg.; cholesterol - 23 mg.; fiber - 0 gm.

ADA exchange value: 1 medium-fat meat

Vegetable Cheese Herb Spread

This is perfect for stuffing in celery sticks or spreading on cucumbers.

7 1/2 oz. dry-curd cottage cheese (or hoop cheese)
4 oz. shredded mozzarella cheese
1/2 tsp. herb blend
1 carrot, sliced
2 celery stalks, chopped large

1. Put all ingredients in food processor and process with steel blade until smooth.
2. Place in an air-tight container and refrigerate.

Serves 6.

Nutrient information per serving:

calories - 76; protein - 9 gm.; carbohydrate - 3 gm.; fat - 3 gm.; saturated fat - 2 gm.; percentage of calories from fat - 36; sodium - 107 mg.; cholesterol - 12 mg.; fiber - 1 gm.

ADA exchange value: 1 lean meat

Eggplant Appetizer

1 large eggplant, unpeeled unless skin is leathery,
 diced into 1/2-inch pieces.
1 cup tomatoes, diced
2 Tbsp. tomato paste
2 cloves garlic, crushed
1 Tbsp. lemon juice
1 tsp. fructose or sugar
2 tsp. ground cumin
1 Tbsp. capers
1/4 tsp. cayenne pepper
1 cup water

1. In a large saucepan, boil water and add eggplant. Cook over medium heat until tender; drain and mash.
2. Add remaining ingredients and combine well.
3. Chill several hours or overnight.
4. Serve as a garnish, relish, or with crackers or bread.

Serves 12.

Nutrient information per serving:

calories - 11; protein - 0 gm.; carbohydrate - 1gm.; fat - 0 gm.; saturated fat - 0gm.; percentage of calories from fat - 0; sodium - 0 mg.; cholesterol - 0 mg.; fiber - 0 gm.

ADA exchange value: Free

Chicken Drumettes

30 chicken drumettes
1 cup light soy sauce
2 Tbsp. sugar
1 1/2 tsp. ground ginger
1/2 tsp. five-spice powder
4 green onions, sliced thin

1. Blanche chicken drumettes in boiling water for 5 minutes. Rinse in cold water and remove skins.
2. Mix all ingredients together, except chicken.
3. Add chicken to marinade, cover, and refrigerate overnight.
4. Preheat oven to 350°. Place chicken on baking sheet that has been sprayed with nonstick spray and bake chicken 45 minutes. Serve hot or cold.

Serves 6.

Nutrient information per serving:

calories - 157; protein - 24 gm.; carbohydrate - 8 gm.; fat - 3 gm.; saturated fat - 1gm.; percentage of calories from fat - 17; sodium - 1092 mg.; cholesterol - 59 mg.; fiber - 0 gm.

ADA exchange value: 3 lean meat, 1/2 fruit

Phyllo Goat Cheese Appetizer

This makes an excellent first course.

6 sheets phyllo dough
1 recipe Goat Cheese Spread (page 54)
1 recipe Tri Color Peppers (page 199)

1. Take one sheet phyllo dough at a time, spraying it lightly with olive-oil spray. Fold over and spray lightly again. Fold again. Place 2 oz. of goat cheese spread in the center and fold over, spraying lightly again with olive oil. Fold over once more and spray again.
2. Repeat step 1 make a total of six . Place on baking sheet sprayed with olive oil and bake at 350° for 30 minutes.
3. Make Tri Color Peppers.
4. Place each phyllo square on a salad plate and spoon peppers along side.

Serves 6.

Nutrient information per serving:

calories - 179; protein - 11 gm.; carbohydrate - 23 gm.; fat - 5 gm.; saturated fat - 3 gm.; percentage of calories from fat - 23; sodium - 539 mg.; cholesterol - 23 mg.; fiber - 1 gm.

ADA exchange value: 1 medium fat meat, 1 starch, 1 vegetable

Crab Cakes

These crab cakes can be served as an appetizer or finger food, or on a plate atop lettuce leaves as a first course.

1 pound fresh crab meat (or imitation if fresh is not available)
1/2 cup bread crumbs
1/2 tsp. herb salt blend (page 42)
2 egg whites
2 Tbsp. low-calorie mayonnaise
2 Tbsp. 1% milk
2 Tbsp. green onion, minced
1 Tbsp. fresh chopped parsley
1 tsp. Worcestershire sauce
1 tsp. Dijon mustard
Dash Tabasco sauce
1/4 tsp. ground white pepper
2/3 cup flour
1/2 tsp. paprika
1/8 tsp. cayenne pepper
2 lemons, cut in wedges

1. In a large bowl, combine crab, bread crumbs, herb blend, egg whites, mayonnaise, milk, onion, parsley, Worcestershire sauce, mustard, Tabasco, and pepper.
2. Mix flour, paprika, and cayenne pepper together.
3. Divide first mixture into 12 balls. Flatten to make cakes and then dip each in flour mixture to coat.
4. In a large nonstick skillet sprayed with nonstick spray, fry each cake 2 minutes on each side.
5. Serve with lemon wedges.

Serves 6.

Nutrient information per serving:

calories - 161; protein - 11 gm.; carbohydrate - 17 gm.; fat - 5 gm.; saturated fat - 1 gm.; percentage of calories from fat - 28; sodium - 220 mg.; cholesterol - 44 mg.; fiber - 1 gm.

ADA exchange value: 1 lean meat, 1 starch/bread, 1 fat

Country Pate Without Liver

For the times you want to serve a pate, but aren't sure if everyone likes liver, this pate is just right. Excellent served with mustard and a spicy tomato sauce, you can make it a day ahead, or you can freeze it to have on hand when needed. It's a great appetizer for company.

1 pound chicken breast, skinned, boned, and ground
1/2 pound chicken thighs, boned and ground
1/2 pound pork, trimmed of all fat and ground
1 medium onion, chopped
2 Tbsp. fresh chopped parsley
1 tsp. fresh ground black pepper
1/2 tsp. ground ginger
1/4 tsp. ground cloves
1/4 tsp. cinnamon
1 tsp. Worcestershire sauce
1/4 tsp. cayenne pepper
1 Tbsp. cognac
2 Tbsp. sherry or Madeira

1. Combine all ingredients well.
2. Spray a nonstick loaf pan with nonstick spray and press mixture into it. Cover with foil and bake in preheated oven at 350° for one hour.

Serves 10.

Nutrient information per serving:

calories - 188; protein - 25 gm.; carbohydrate - 1 gm.; fat - 7 gm.; saturated fat - 2 gm.; percentage of calories from fat - 37; sodium - 65 mg.; cholesterol - 73 mg.; fiber - 0 gm.

ADA exchange value: 3 lean meat

Spinach And Chicken Pate

This makes an excellent appetizer or main course for a luncheon or light supper. Just serve it with a big green salad.

1 shallot
10-oz. pkg. frozen spinach thawed, with water squeezed out
1 pound boned skinned chicken breast, chopped
1 Tbsp. arrowroot
1 cup 1% milk
1/4 tsp. nutmeg
1 Tbsp. fresh tarragon (or 1/2 Tbsp. dried)
1/2 tsp. cayenne pepper
1/2 tsp. fresh ground black pepper
1/4 tsp. salt
8 oz. egg substitute

1. In food processor with steel blade, drop shallots and garlic while the processor is running and mince well.
2. Add remaining ingredients to the processor and pulse on and off until all is mixed well.
3. Put mixture in a loaf pan and cover with foil.
4. Bake in preheated oven at 375° for 45 minutes. Let cool 10 minutes before unmolding.

Serves 6.

Nutrient information per serving:

calories - 180; protein - 30 gm.; carbohydrate - 7 gm.; fat - 3 gm.; saturated fat - 1 gm.; percentage of calories from fat - 18; sodium - 296 mg.; cholesterol - 60 mg.; fiber - 2 gm.

ADA exchange value: 3 lean meat, 1 vegetable

Chicken-Liver Pate

This is almost like a pate I used to make that was very high in fat. With a few modifications, however, it still tastes great, and the fat is gone. Serve with water crackers or melba toast.

4 green onions, including tops, chopped
2 Tbsp. margarine
1 1/2 lbs. chicken livers
1/2 tsp. salt
2 tsp. dry mustard
1/2 tsp. ground nutmeg
1/4 tsp. ground cloves
16 oz. nonfat cream cheese
1/4 cup cognac

1. In a large skillet, melt margarine. Add onions and saute until tender.
2. Add chicken livers, salt, mustard, nutmeg, and cloves. Cover and cook over low heat for 10 to 15 minutes or until livers are well cooked.
3. Place in food processor with steel blade and process until smooth.
4. While processor is running, add nonfat cream cheese; then add cognac.
5. Pour the mixture onto a pate tureen or a souffle dish. Chill for 12 to 24 hours before serving.

Serves 16.

Nutrient information per serving:

calories - 62; protein - 7 gm.; carbohydrate - 1 gm.; fat - 2 gm.; saturated fat - 1 gm.; percentage of calories from fat - 30; sodium - 261 mg.; cholesterol - 87 mg.; fiber - 0 gm.

ADA exchange value: 1 lean meat

Mexican Banana Salsa

A variation on traditional Mexican salsa, this makes an excellent sauce to use with grilled shrimp. The taste is both piquant and sweet. Try this the next time you want to make a really interesting hot shrimp appetizer.

1 large ripe, firm banana, peeled and diced
1/4 red sweet pepper, diced
1/4 sweet green pepper, diced
2 Tbsp. fresh mint or cilantro, chopped
1 scallion, trimmed and chopped fine
1 1/2 Tbsp. fresh lime juice
1 Tbsp. brown sugar
1 1/2 tsp. minced gingerroot
1 1/2 tsp. olive oil
1 Tbsp. minced Jalapeno pepper

1. Combine all ingredients; toss lightly to mix.
2. Serve chilled. Make 1 1/2 cups (one serving = 1 Tbsp).

Nutrient information per serving:

calories - 10; protein - 0 gm.; carbohydrate - 2 gm.; fat - 0 gm.; saturated fat - 0 gm.; percentage of calories from fat - 0; sodium - 0 mg.; cholesterol - 0 mg.; fiber - 1 gm.

ADA exchange value: 1/2 fruit

SOUPS

Mushroom And Barley Soup

1 medium onion, chopped
1 clove garlic, minced
1 tsp. basil, crushed
6 cups low-salt beef broth
1 cup barley
1/2 tsp. Worcestershire sauce
1/8 tsp. pepper
8 oz. mushrooms, sliced
1/2 cup shredded carrots
2 Tbsp. cornstarch mixed with 2 Tbsp. water
1 Tbsp. fresh chopped parsley

1. In a large cast-iron pot sprayed with nonstick spray, saute onion and garlic until soft.
2. Add basil and beef broth and bring to a boil.
3. Add barley, Worcestershire sauce, and pepper. Cover and simmer 15 minutes.
4. Add mushrooms and carrots. Cover and simmer 10 minutes more.
5. Uncover and add cornstarch mixture and cook until thick. Add parsley and serve.

Serves 4.

Nutrient information per serving:

calories - 246; protein - 12 gm.; carbohydrate - 49 gm.; fat - 1 gm.; saturated fat - 1 gm.; percentage of calories from fat - 0; sodium - 374 mg.; cholesterol - 6 mg.; fiber - 5 gm.

ADA exchange value: 3 starch/bread, 1 vegetable

Yogurt Cucumber Soup

1 32-oz. container nonfat plain yogurt
1 large cucumber, diced
1/2 cup diced walnuts
1 tsp. fresh dill (or 1/2 tsp. dried dill weed)
1/2 tsp. freshly ground white pepper
1/8 tsp. salt
Fresh dill to garnish

1. Mix all ingredients in a large bowl, cover, and refrigerate for at least 1 hour.
2. Garnish with fresh dill and serve.

Serves 6.

Nutrient information per serving:

calories - 156; protein - 11 gm.; carbohydrate - 17 gm.; fat - 5 gm.; saturated fat - 0 gm.; percentage of calories from fat - 30; sodium - 123 mg.; cholesterol - 0mg.; fiber - 1 gm.

ADA exchange value: 1 milk, 1 vegetable, 1 fat

Gazpacho

1 cup cucumber, diced
1 green bell pepper, seeded and diced
1 4-oz. can diced green chilies, drained
1 46-oz. can tomato juice
1/2 tsp. Worcestershire sauce
1 1/2 cup diced tomatoes
1 Tbsp. fresh chopped cilantro
1 Tbsp. fresh chopped oregano
2 green onions, diced
1/8 tsp. cayenne pepper

1. Combine all ingredients. Put half of the mixture into a food processor and blend until smooth.
2. Combine the two mixtures in a large bowl. Cover and refrigerate at least one hour before serving.

Serves 6.

Nutrient information per serving:

calories - 61; protein - 3 gm.; carbohydrate - 15 gm.; fat - 0 gm.; saturated fat - 0 gm.; percentage of calories from fat - 1; sodium - 1058 mg.; cholesterol - 0 mg.; fiber - 4 gm.

ADA exchange value: 3 vegetables

Gazpacho With An Island Flavor

When you want to sneak away to Hawaii but just can't go, here's an avocado and papaya chilled soup that can make you think you've been there.

1 cup canned tomato juice
1 cup canned unsweetened pineapple juice
1 ripe papaya, seeds removed, diced
1 ripe, firm avocado, peeled, pit removed, diced
1 large tomato, peeled and chopped
1 green bell pepper, finely diced
1/2 red onion, finely diced
1/4 cup fresh lime juice
8 dashes Tabasco sauce
1/4 cup finely chopped fresh cilantro
Salt and freshly ground black pepper to taste

1. Gently mix all ingredients in large bowl.
2. Cover and refrigerate 2 hours before serving. Serve cold.

Serves 6 (yield is 5 cups).

Nutrient information per serving:

calories - 108; protein - 2 gm.; carbohydrate - 16 gm.; fat - 8 gm.; saturated fat - 2 gm.; percentage of calories from fat - 30; sodium - 157 mg.; cholesterol - 0 mg.; fiber - 4 gm.

ADA exchange value: 1 fruit

Cranberry Cinnamon Soup

Before we leave the chilled soups, here's one sure to please any readers in New England. This is beautiful for serving at the holidays and it blends tartness and sweetness into a real taste treat.

4 cups fresh cranberries
3 cups water
1 cup fructose
3 inches stick cinnamon
1/4 tsp. ground cloves
2 Tbsp. lemon juice
1 Tbsp. orange peel, shredded fine
Orange peel curl to garnish
Mint leaves to garnish

1. Combine cranberries, water, sugar, cinnamon, and cloves in a 3-quart saucepan. Simmer, uncovered, for 5 minutes or until at least half the cranberries have popped open. Remove from heat.
2. Stir in lemon juice and orange peel. Cool. Cover and chill for 4 to 24 hours. Remove cinnamon stick and serve. Ladle into soup bowls and top with orange peel curl and mint leaves for a truly festive look.

Makes 8 2/4 cup servings.

Nutrient information per serving:

calories - 190; protein - 9 gm.; carbohydrate - 50 gm.; fat - 0 gm.; saturated fat - 0 gm.; percentage of calories from fat - 0; sodium - 4 mg.; cholesterol - 0 mg.; fiber - 3 gm.

ADA exchange value: 1 fruit

Corn Soup

1/2 medium onion, chopped
6 cups low-sodium chicken broth
2 cups corn kernels
1 tsp. ground ginger
1/2 tsp. herb salt blend (page 42)
1/4 tsp. freshly ground pepper
2 Tbsp. low-sodium soy sauce
2 Tbsp. water
1 Tbsp. cornstarch
4 egg whites
2 green onions, sliced thin

1. In a large cast-iron pot sprayed with nonstick spray, add onions and saute until soft.
2. Add chicken broth and bring to a boil. Stir in corn, ginger, herb salt, and pepper. Cover, reduce heat, and simmer until hot.
3. Combine soy sauce, water, and cornstarch and slowly add to soup, stirring constantly until soup is thickened. (If you are making the soup ahead of time, hold the preparation at this point.)
4. Beat eggs with green onion, and gradually add mixture to soup, stirring just until eggs are set.
5. Serve immediately.

Serves 6.

Nutrient information per serving:

calories - 86; protein - 5 gm.; carbohydrate - 15 gm.; fat - 1 gm.; saturated fat - 0 gm.; percentage of calories from fat - 14; sodium - 1911 mg.; cholesterol - 1 mg.; fiber - 3 gm.

ADA exchange value: 1 starch/bread, 1/2 lean meat

Tomato Herb Bouillon

Here's a really tasty, fast, and easy starter bouillon that's sure to please.

1 tsp. beef-flavored bouillon granules
1 cup hot water
3 cups no-salt-added tomato juice
2 Tbsp. fresh parsley, chopped
1 Tbsp. lemon juice
1 tsp. low-sodium Worcestershire sauce
1/2 tsp. dried whole rosemary
1/2 tsp. dried whole thyme
1/4 tsp. pepper
lemon slices to garnish

1. Dissolve bouillon in hot water.
2. Add tomato juice and next six ingredients. Microwave on high for 3 to 5 minutes or until mixture is hot.
3. Ladle bouillon into soup bowls and garnish with lemon.

Makes 4 cups.

Nutrient information per serving:

calories - 43; protein - 2 gm.; carbohydrate - 10 gm.; fat - 0.3 gm.; saturated fat - 0 gm.; percentage of calories from fat - 6; sodium - 262 mg.; cholesterol - 0 mg.; fiber - 0 gm.

ADA exchange value: 1/2 lean meat, 1/2 fruit

Golden Squash Soup

Here's a soup that's pleasing not only to the palate,but to the eye, too. It may take a little longer to prepare than our other recipes, but, believe me, it's worth the extra time.

2 cups acorn or butternut squash, cooked and mashed
3 onions, chopped
1 cup celery, chopped
1 clove garlic, minced
1/2 tsp. rosemary
1 qt. low-sodium, low-fat chicken broth
1/4 tsp. freshly ground black pepper
2 cups skim milk
Nutmeg to garnish

1. Combine all ingredients, except milk, in a soup pot. Cook until onions and celery are soft.
2. Remove from heat, add milk, sprinkle with nutmeg.

Serves 6.

Nutrient information per serving:

calories - 66; protein - 5 gm.; carbohydrate - 0 gm.; fat - 1 gm.; saturated fat - 0 gm.; percentage of calories from fat - 14; sodium - 69 mg.; cholesterol - 1 mg.; fiber - 0 gm.

ADA exchange value: 1 starch/bread, 1/2 lean meat

SALADS

Free-Food Salad

With your favorite lettuce, celery, onion, radishes, peppers, fresh herbs, and vinegars, you can create wonderful salads that are filling and free! If you chop everything up finely and toss with seasoned rice-wine vinegar, you have a great tasting free treat. You can make this your dinner salad or have a large serving as your entire lunch. You can also use this as a base to make other very-low-calorie salads.

SPECIAL HERB BLEND DRESSING

1/2 cup red-wine vinegar
1/2 tsp. orange juice concentrate
1/2 tsp. dried oregano
1/4 tsp. dried basil
1/4 tsp. dried tarragon
1/2 tsp. dry mustard
1/4 tsp. black pepper
1/2 tsp. garlic, minced
3/4 tsp. Worcestershire sauce
1/4 cup wheat or oat bran
1/2 cup rice-wine vinegar

1. Combine all ingredients in blender and blend at top speed for 2 minutes.
2. Chill and serve.

Makes 16 tablespoons(1 serving = 1 tablespoon).

Nutrient information per serving:

calories - 4; protein - trace; carbohydrate - 1 gm.; fat - trace; saturated fat - 0 gm.; percentage of calories from fat - trace; sodium - 10 mg.; cholesterol - 0 mg.; fiber - 0 gm.

ADA exchange value: free

Fruit Salad With Dressing

You can use a variety of fruits for this salad, but always choose fresh when possible. If you can only get frozen, be sure no sugar has been added. If you are using canned fruits, buy the kind canned in fruit juice with no sugar added.

2 apples, cored and sliced
3 apricots, quartered
1 cantaloupe, cut in pieces
2 cups strawberries
1 head iceberg lettuce, cut into cubes

1. Mix all ingredients.
2. Make salad dressing and pour over fruit.
3. Toss well.

Serves 6.

DRESSING

2/3 cup white-wine vinegar
2/3 cup fruit nectar
1/4 tsp. marjoram
1/2 tsp. ground nutmeg
1/2 tsp. orange peel
1/4 tsp. lemon peel
2 tsp. chervil

Place all ingredients in a container and shake well.

Nutrient information per serving:

calories - 106; protein - 2 gm.; carbohydrate - 26 gm.; fat - 1 gm.; saturated fat - 0 gm.; percentage of calories from fat - 7; sodium - 15 mg.; cholesterol - 0 mg.; fiber - 4 gm.

ADA exchange value: 2 fruit

Cucumber And Tomatoes In Lettuce Cups

6 lettuce leaves (or cups)
2 medium ripe tomatoes, diced
1 cucumber, diced
1/2 tsp. herb salt
1 Tbsp. basil chopped
2 Tbsp. wine vinegar

1. Place lettuce cups on 6 plates or on a large platter.
2. Mix remaining ingredients and place in lettuce cups.
3. Serve or hold in refrigerator until you are ready to serve.

Serves 6.

Nutrient information per serving:

calories - 20; protein - 1 gm.; carbohydrate - 4 gm.; fat - 0 gm.; saturated fat - 0 gm.; percentage of calories from fat - 1; sodium - 7 mg.; cholesterol - 0 mg.; fiber - 2 gm.

ADA exchange value: 1 vegetable

Dilled Shrimp Salad

1 lb. shrimp, cooked, cleaned,and deveined
1/2 onion, peeled and sliced
1 can water chestnuts, sliced (5 oz.)
4 Tbsp. special herb-blend dressing (page 76)
2 Tbsp. fresh dillweed, chopped (or 1 tsp. dried)
1 head romaine lettuce
3 tomatoes
4 oz. mushrooms, sliced
Fresh parsley to garnish

1. Drain and chill shrimp.
2. Toss shrimp, onion, water chestnuts, and dressing. Sprinkle with dill.
3. Serve on romaine lettuce. Surround with sliced tomatoes and mushrooms. Garnish with parsley.

Serves 10.

Nutrient information per serving:

calories - 85; protein - 12 gm.; carbohydrate - 7 gm.; fat - 1 gm.; saturated fat - 0 gm.; percentage of calories from fat - 6; sodium - 118 mg.; cholesterol - 0 mg.; fiber - 2 gm.

ADA exchange value: 1 lean meat, 1 vegetable

Rice Salad Oriental

2 cups cooked brown rice
1 Tbsp. instant onion, toasted
1/2 cup radishes, sliced
1/2 green pepper, sliced
2 small celery stalks, sliced
4 tsp. low-sodium soy sauce
1 Tbsp. freshly chopped cilantro
1/4 tsp. ground ginger
1/8 tsp. garlic powder
4 Tbsp. seasoned rice-wine vinegar
1 head red leaf lettuce, keep out 6 leaves and chop the rest

1. Mix all the ingredients, except the lettuce, in a large bowl. Toss well to mix. Cover and refrigerate for 1 hour.
2. Toss in the chopped lettuce. Line a salad bowl with remaining lettuce leaves and place the mixture in the center.

Serves 6.

Nutrient information per serving:

calories - 45; protein - 1 gm.; carbohydrate - 10 gm.; fat - 0 gm.; saturated fat - 0 gm.; percentage of calories from fat - 4; sodium - 219 mg.; cholesterol - 0 mg.; fiber - 1 gm.

ADA exchange value: 3/4 starch/bread, 1 vegetable

Coleslaw With Caraway

3 cups finely shredded cabbage
2 tsp. Beau Monde seasoning
2 tsp. sugar
1/2 tsp. hot mustard
1 Tbsp. finely chopped chives
2 Tbsp. seasoned rice-wine vinegar
1/2 cup nonfat sour cream
1 tsp. crushed caraway seed

1. Place cabbage in a large bowl.
2. Mix remaining ingredients and pour over cabbage. Toss well.
3. Chill until ready to serve.

Serves 6.

Nutrient information per serving:

calories - 35; protein - 2 gm.; carbohydrate - 7 gm.; fat - 0 gm.; saturated fat - 0 gm.; percentage of calories from fat - 3; sodium - 39 mg.; cholesterol - 0 mg.; fiber - 1 gm.

ADA exchange value: 1 vegetable

Cabbage-Carrot Coleslaw

3 Tbsp. reduced-fat mayonnaise
3 Tbsp. plain, nonfat yogurt
1 Tbsp. Dijon mustard
2 tsp. cider vinegar
1 tsp. sugar
1/2 tsp. caraway seed
Salt and freshly ground black pepper to taste
2 cups shredded red cabbage
2 cups shredded green cabbage
1 cup grated carrots

1. In large bowl, combine mayonnaise, yogurt, mustard, vinegar, sugar, and caraway seed.
2. Add salt and pepper.
3. Add cabbage and carrots and toss well.

Serve right away or chill and serve within 2 hours.

Serves 4.

Nutrient information per serving:

calories - 70; protein - 2 gm.; carbohydrate - 10 gm.; fat - 3 gm.; saturated fat - 0 gm.; percentage of calories from fat - 13; sodium - 37 mg.; cholesterol - 4 mg.; fiber - 1 gm.

ADA exchange value: 1 vegetable

Cumin-Carrot Slaw

1 lb. carrots, peeled and coarsely grated (about 6 carrots)
1/2 cup chopped fresh parsley
1 Tbsp. fresh lemon juice
1 Tbsp. olive oil (preferably extra virgin)
1 clove garlic, minced
1/2 tsp. ground cumin
Salt and freshly ground black pepper to taste

Toss all ingredients in a medium-sized bowl. This salad is ready to serve.

Serves 4.

Nutrient information per serving:

calories - 85; protein - 1 gm.; carbohydrate - 13 gm.; fat - 3.4 gm.; saturated fat - 0 gm.; percentage of calories from fat - 30; sodium - 43 mg.; cholesterol - 0 mg.; fiber - 1 gm.

ADA exchange value: 1 vegetable

Spinach, Raspberry, and Walnut Salad

1 1/2 lb. fresh spinach, washed and dried
1 cup fresh raspberries
1/4 cup chopped walnuts
1 Tbsp. chopped tarragon
1/4 cup raspberry vinegar
1/2 cup raspberry juice

1. Tear spinach into small pieces.
2. In a salad bowl, place spinach, raspberries, tarragon, and walnuts.
3. Mix together vinegar and raspberry juice. Pour over salad and toss to coat.

Serves 6.

Nutrient information per serving:

calories - 74; protein - 4 gm.; carbohydrate - 11 gm.; fat - 3 gm.; saturated fat - 0 gm.; percentage of calories from fat - 38; sodium - 90 mg.; cholesterol - 0 mg.; fiber - 6 gm.

ADA exchange value: 2 vegetable, 1/2 fat

Bibb Lettuce With Radishes

1 head bibb lettuce, washed, dried, and torn into medium-sized pieces
12 radishes sliced thin

VINAIGRETTE DRESSING

1 Tbsp. olive oil
3 Tbsp. herb wine vinegar
1/2 tsp. dip blend (page 44)
2 Tbsp. water
1 tsp. Dijon mustard
1/8 tsp. freshly ground black pepper

1. Put lettuce and radishes into a salad bowl.
2. Combine vinaigrette ingredients. Mix well.
3. Toss dressing into lettuce.

Serves 6.

Nutrient information per serving:

calories - 31; protein - 1 gm.; carbohydrate - 2 gm.; fat - 2 gm.; saturated fat - 0 gm.; percentage of calories from fat - 70; sodium - 16 mg.; cholesterol - 0 mg.; fiber - 1 gm.

ADA exchange value: 1 vegetable, 1/2 fat

Spinach And Feta Salad

1 bunch fresh spinach, washed, dried, and torn into small pieces
1/4 cup diced walnuts
1/4 cup red-wine vinegar
1/4 cup water
2 Tbsp. basil, chopped
1/2 cup feta cheese spread (recipe on page 54)
1/2 tsp. freshly ground black pepper

1. Place spinach and walnuts in large salad bowl.
2. Mix the remaining ingredients.
3. Pour dressing over salad and toss well to coat.

Serves 6.

Nutrient information per serving:

calories - 48; protein - 4 gm.; carbohydrate - 3 gm.; fat - 3 gm.; saturated fat - 0 gm.; percentage of calories from fat - 54; sodium - 50 mg.; cholesterol - 1 mg.; fiber - 2 gm.

ADA exchange value: 1 vegetable

EGGS

Crustless Quiche

This is great as an appetizer or as part of a brunch buffet.

8 oz. egg substitute
4 egg whites
1/2 cup flour
1 tsp. baking powder
1 tsp. Greek blend (page 43)
2 cups nonfat cottage cheese
1 cup green chilies, chopped
4 oz. Monterey Jack cheese, grated
6 oz. Mozzarella cheese, grated

1. Spray a 9 x 13-inch baking dish with nonstick spray. Preheat oven to 400°.
2. Put egg substitute, egg whites, flour, baking powder, Greek blend, and cottage cheese into work bowl of food processor and process with a steel blade until well blended and smooth.
3. Add green chilies and cheese to processor and pulse on and off until just blended.
4. Pour into baking dish and bake 15 minutes. Lower heat to 350° and bake 30 minutes longer. Cool 10 minutes and cut into 1-inch squares.

Serves 8.

Nutrient information per serving:

calories - 144; protein - 17 gm.; carbohydrate - 9 gm.; fat - 4 gm.; saturated fat - 2 gm.; percentage of calories from fat - 23; sodium - 492 mg.; cholesterol - 14 mg.; fiber - 0 gm.

ADA exchange value: 1/2 starch/bread, 2 lean meat

Potato Fritata

Top with low-fat sour cream and salsa for extra zip.

3 medium russet potatoes, cut into thin slices
1/4 tsp. paprika
1 tsp. Italian seasoning
4 whole eggs plus 8 egg whites, beaten together
2 oz. freshly grated Parmesan cheese

1. Spray a 10-inch skillet with olive-oil spray and heat.
2. Toss potatoes with seasonings, blending well. Put in hot skillet and cook until brown on the bottom.
3. Spray the top of the potatoes with olive oil spray, turn over, and cook until light brown.
4. Combine cheese and eggs, pour over potatoes, and reduce heat to medium. Lift the potatoes and let some of the egg mixture go underneath them. Add 2 tablespoons of water, cover, reduce heat to low, and cook until eggs are set (about 8 to 10 minutes).

Serves 4.

Nutrient information per serving:

calories - 262; protein - 20 gm.; carbohydrate - 22 gm.; fat - 10 gm.; saturated fat - 4 gm.; percentage of calories from fat - 34; sodium - 438 mg.; cholesterol - 285 mg.; fiber - 1 gm.

ADA exchange value: 2 lean meat, 1 1/2 starch/bread, 1 fat

Veggie Omelette

It's okay to have eggs occasionally. Just omit a couple egg yolks.

2 egg whites
1 egg
1 Tbsp. cold water
1 tsp. fresh dillweed, or 1/2 tsp. dried
1/2 cup bean sprouts
2 Tbsp. sliced mushrooms
2 Tbsp. chopped onions
2 Tbsp. chopped green pepper
1/2 of 1 tomato, chopped
Freshly ground black pepper to taste
Sprigs fresh parsley to garnish

1. Whisk egg whites, egg, water, and dillweed together until foamy.
2. Heat a nonstick omelette pan very hot.
3. Spray pan with cooking spray. Pour in eggs and tilt pan to cover bottom evenly. (Use a spatula to move the mixture so it cooks evenly.)
4. When eggs are cooked, fill one side of the omelette with the chopped vegetables. Lift the other side of the omelette to fold it over the top.
5. Sprinkle with black pepper. Move to plate, garnish with parsley, and serve.

Nutrient information per serving:

calories - 192; protein - 19 gm.; carbohydrate - 18 gm.; fat - 6 gm.; saturated fat - 2 gm.; percentage of calories from fat - 28; sodium - 121 mg.; cholesterol - 285 mg.; fiber - 1 gm.

ADA exchange value: 2 lean meat, 1/2 vegetable, 1 fat

PASTA

Fettuccine With Artichokes And Tomatoes

1 medium onion, chopped
2 carrots, cut in quarters, then into thin strips
2 28-oz. cans whole or diced tomatoes
2 tsp. fresh thyme (1/2 tsp. dried)
2 tsp. fresh rosemary, chopped (1/2 tsp. dried)
1/4 tsp. freshly ground black pepper
2 9-oz. pkgs. frozen artichoke hearts, thawed
2 oz. freshly grated Parmesan cheese
1 lb. fettuccine, cooked al dente

1. In a large cast-iron pot or Dutch oven sprayed with olive-oil spray, saute onions until soft.
2. Add carrots, tomatoes with juice (if you are using whole tomatoes, chop them), thyme, rosemary, and pepper. Simmer uncovered 25 minutes.
3. Cut the artichokes in quarters and add them to the sauce. Simmer for 15 minutes, uncovered.
4. Add the fettuccine and Parmesan and toss.

Serves 8.

Nutrient information per serving:

calories - 245; protein - 10 gm.; carbohydrate - 45 gm.; fat - 3 gm.; saturated fat - 1 gm.; percentage of calories from fat - 11; sodium - 385 mg.; cholesterol - 6 mg.; fiber - 5 gm.

ADA exchange value: 2 starch/bread, 2 vegetable, 1/2 lean meat

Fresh Basil Marinara With Mosticiolli

This is not only quick and easy, but it is great to have cold the next day for lunch.

2 28-oz. cans whole plum tomatoes with basil
1 onion diced
1 clove garlic, diced
1/2 tsp. freshly ground black pepper
1/2 tsp. ground red pepper
1 lb. mostaccioli, cooked al dente
1/2 cup freshly chopped parsley
3 Tbsp. freshly sliced basil
2 oz. freshly grated Parmesan cheese

1. Place tomatoes in a food processor or blender. Process until smooth.
2. Spray a large skillet with olive oil and heat.
3. Add onions and garlic and saute until soft.
4. Add tomatoes and pepper. Simmer 10 minutes uncovered.
5. Add mostaccioli to sauce and stir until heated through.
6. Toss in fresh basil, parsley, and Parmesan cheese.

Serves 6.

Nutrient information per serving:

calories - 307; protein - 13 gm.; carbohydrate - 58 gm.; fat - 4 gm.; saturated fat - 2 gm.; percentage of calories from fat - 13; sodium - 631 mg.; cholesterol - 7 mg.; fiber - 6 gm.

ADA exchange value: 3 starch/bread, 2 vegetable, 1 lean meat

Macaroni And Cheese

We can still enjoy this old family favorite with only a few minor alterations!

1 lb. elbow macaroni, uncooked
2 Tbsp. cornstarch
1 1/2 cups skim milk
1/2 tsp. dry mustard
1/4 tsp. white ground pepper
1 tsp. Worcestershire sauce
1/2 basic herb blend (page 44)
1/4 tsp. cayenne pepper
2 cups reduced-fat sharp cheddar cheese, grated
Garnish with freshly chopped parsley and paprika

1. In a large pasta pot, bring water to a boil. Add pasta and cook until tender. Remove from water, rinse, and set aside.
2. Mix remaining ingredients except cheeses in a large saucepan. Whisk together well, turn on heat, and bring to a simmer, stirring constantly.
3. Add cheese and stir until all is melted.
4. Stir in macaroni. You can either serve this dish right away, or you can put it in a baking dish and keep it in a warm oven until you are ready to serve. Garnish with freshly chopped parsley and paprika.

Serves 8.

Nutrient information per serving:

calories - 202; protein - 10 gm.; carbohydrate - 34 gm.; fat - 2 gm.; saturated fat - 0 gm.; percentage of calories from fat - 10; sodium - 110 mg.; cholesterol - 6 mg.; fiber - 1 gm.

ADA exchange value: 2 starch/bread, 1 medium-fat meat

Colorful Peppers

4 large bell peppers, cut in half, seeded, and washed (or you can use red or yellow peppers for variety)
2 cups small pasta shells, cooked al dente
1/4 cup fresh basil chopped
3 garlic cloves minced
2 Tbsp. chopped chives
4 Roma tomatoes, chopped
2 shallots, minced
2 cups grated mozzarella cheese
1/4 tsp. freshly ground black pepper

1. Place pepper halves in a baking dish sprayed with nonstick spray.
2. Mix remaining ingredients well and fill pepper halves.
3. Bake at 350° for 40 minutes.

Serves 8.

Nutrient information per serving:

calories - 131; protein - 9 gm.; carbohydrate - 13 gm.; fat - 5 gm.; saturated fat - 3 gm.; percentage of calories from fat - 38; sodium - 137 mg.; cholesterol - 16 mg.; fiber - 2 gm.

ADA exchange value: 1 medium-fat meat, 1 starch/bread, 1 vegetable

Vermicelli With Tomato Clam Sauce

4 cloves garlic, chopped
1 onion, chopped
2 carrots, chopped
1/2 cup red wine (or dry vermouth)
2 28-oz. cans diced tomatoes with juice
1 Tbsp. freshly chopped oregano (1 tsp. dried)
1 Tbsp. freshly chopped thyme (1/2 tsp. dried)
1/4 tsp. freshly ground black pepper
1 2-oz. can chopped clams, drained
1 Tbsp. freshly chopped parsley
1 lb. Vermicelli, cooked al dente

1. In a large skillet sprayed with olive oil, saute onion, garlic, and carrots until soft.
2. Add red wine, bring to a boil. Add tomatoes, oregano, thyme, and pepper. Simmer uncovered for 25 minutes.
3. Add clams and parsley, stirring well. Pour sauce on vermicelli and toss.

Serves 8.

Nutrient information per serving:

calories - 252; protein - 14 gm.; carbohydrate - 43 gm.; fat - 2 gm.; saturated fat - 0 gm.; percentage of calories from fat - 0; sodium - 263 mg.; cholesterol - 20 mg.; fiber - 4 gm.

ADA exchange value: 2 starch/bread, 2 lean meat, 1 vegetable

Vermicelli With Herb Sauce

You can have this on the table in the time it takes to cook the pasta!

1 lb. vermicelli
1 8-oz. pkg. nonfat cream cheese
1 tsp. basic herb blend (page 44)
1 clove garlic, chopped
1/2 tsp. freshly ground pepper
1/8 tsp. cayenne pepper
3/4 cup boiling water
2 oz. freshly grated Parmesan cheese
Freshly chopped parsley to garnish

1. In a large pasta pot, cook vermicelli al dente.
2. While vermicelli is cooking, put all other ingredients into food processor or blender. Blend until smooth.
3. Toss sauce in pasta after draining pasta well.
4. Garnish with freshly chopped parsley.

Serves 6.

Nutrient information per serving:

calories - 284; protein - 16 gm.; carbohydrate - 45 gm.; fat - 4 gm.; saturated fat - 2 gm.; percentage of calories from fat - 11; sodium - 402 mg.; cholesterol - 14 mg.; fiber - 1 gm.

ADA exchange value: 3 starch/bread, 1 lean meat

Rotini With Dilled Lemon Sauce

This is a perfect side dish for lemon chicken.

2 cups skim milk
3 Tbsp. cornstarch
1/2 tsp. freshly ground white pepper
1 tsp. caraway seed
1/2 cup fresh lemon juice
1 tsp. lemon zest
1 tsp. herb salt (page 42)
4 Tbsp. chopped dill weed (2 Tbsp. dried)
1 lb. rotini, cooked al dente

1. Mix skim milk, cornstarch, and white pepper in saucepan. Bring to a boil, then simmer until thick.
2. Add caraway seeds, lemon juice, lemon zest, and dill.
3. Put hot pasta in large pasta bowl and add sauce. Toss.

Serves 8.

Nutrient information per serving:

calories - 180; protein - 7 gm.; carbohydrate - 36 gm.; fat - 1 gm.; saturated fat - 0 gm.; percentage of calories from fat - 0; sodium - 104 mg.; cholesterol - 1 mg.; fiber - 1 gm.

ADA exchange value: 2 starch/bread, 1/4 skim milk

Pasta Salad With Crab And Snow Peas

4 shallots, thinly sliced
1 cup vegetable broth
2 Tbsp. herbed wine vinegar
fresh black pepper, to taste
1 lb. snow peas, strings removed, sliced diagonally
1 Tbsp. freshly chopped basil (1/2 tsp. dried)
2 Tbsp. freshly chopped parsley
1 lb. imitation crab meat
1 lb. radiatori pasta cooked al dente, rinsed in cold water

1. Spray a skillet with olive oil, saute shallots until soft.
2. Add vegetable broth and vinegar. Bring to a boil, reduce heat to simmer. Add snow peas, basil, and pepper. Remove from heat and cool.
3. Pour mixture over pasta. Add parsley and crab to pasta and toss well. Chill before serving.

Serves 8.

Nutrient information per serving:

calories - 221; protein - 13 gm.; carbohydrate - 39 gm.; fat - 1 gm.; saturated fat - 0 gm.; percentage of calories from fat - 5; sodium - 131 mg.; cholesterol - 21 mg.; fiber - 4 gm.

ADA exchange value: 2 starch/bread, 2 lean meat, 1 vegetable

Spaghetti With Basil And Fresh Pine Nuts

2 cloves garlic, crushed
1 cup low-salt chicken broth
1/2 cup shredded basil leaves
1 Tbsp. cornstarch mixed in 1/4 cup chicken broth
3/4 cup pine nuts
2 oz. freshly grated Romano cheese
freshly ground black pepper to taste
1 lb. thick spaghetti, cooked al dente

1. In a large cast-iron pot or Dutch oven, sprayed with olive oil, lightly saute the garlic (approx. 30 seconds).
2. Add chicken broth and bring to a boil. Reduce heat to simmer, add basil. Stir in cornstarch mixture.
3. In a small skillet, toast pine nuts over medium heat.
4. Add pine nuts, cheese, pepper, and spaghetti to broth.

Serves 8.

Nutrient information per serving:

calories - 212; protein - 9 gm.; carbohydrate - 34 gm.; fat - 4 gm.; saturated fat - 2 gm.; percentage of calories from fat - 17; sodium - 161 mg.; cholesterol - 6 mg.; fiber - 1 gm.

ADA exchange value: 2 starch/bread, 1 lean meat

Pasta With Sun-Dried Tomatoes, Rosemary and Thyme

2 shallots, chopped
1 cup dry vermouth
6 small leeks, trimmed, cleaned, and cut into 3/4 inch slices
4 oz. sun-dried tomatoes, steeped in 1/2 cup hot water
2 tsp. fresh rosemary (1/2 tsp. dried)
2 tsp. fresh thyme (1/2 tsp. dried)
1/2 tsp. salt
2 Tbsp. salt
2 Tbsp. fresh lemon juice
2 oz. freshly grated Parmesan cheese
1 lb. gemelli (or other short, tubular pasta), cooked al dente

1. Spray a skillet with olive oil, saute shallots until soft.
2. Add vermouth to skillet and bring to simmer. Add leeks, tomatoes with water, rosemary, thyme, salt, and lemon juice.
3. Place hot pasta in a large bowl and toss with cheese and sauce. Serve immediately.

Serves 8.

Nutrient information per serving:

calories - 216; protein - 8 gm.; carbohydrate - 26 gm.; fat - 3 gm.; saturated fat - 1 gm.; percentage of calories from fat - 12; sodium - 273 mg.; cholesterol - 6 mg.; fiber - 2 gm.

ADA exchange value: 2 starch/bread, 1 vegetable, 1 fat

Linguine And Clams

2 shallots, chopped
2 oz. canned clams with juice
3/4 cup dry vermouth
1/4 tsp. saffron threads, steeped in 3/4 cup hot water
2 Tbsp. chopped chives
2 Tbsp. cornstarch, mixed in 1/4 cup cold water
Freshly ground black pepper to taste
2 oz. freshly grated Romano cheese
1 lb. linguine, cooked al dente

1. In a large skillet sprayed with olive oil, saute shallots until soft.
2. Add clams with juice, vermouth, and saffron to skillet and bring to simmer.
3. Make sure cornstarch is mixed well into water and add to simmering liquid. Stir until thick.
4. Add chives and pepper to mixture.
5. Place hot linguine into pasta bowl and toss with cheese and clam mixture. Serve immediately.

Serves 8.

Nutrient information per serving:

calories - 249; protein - 16 gm.; carbohydrate - 35 gm.; fat - 3 gm.; saturated fat - 1 gm.; percentage of calories from fat - 11; sodium - 167 mg.; cholesterol - 26 mg.; fiber - 1 gm.

ADA exchange value: 2 starch/bread, 2 lean meat

Prosciutto And Tomato Pasta

1 tsp. olive oil
4 small cloves garlic, minced
1/2 lb. Prosciutto ham, diced (all fat removed)
2 28-oz. cans diced tomatoes with juice
2 Tbsp. fresh basil, chopped
1 lb. thick pasta noodles, cooked al dente

1. Heat olive oil in a cast-iron pot or Dutch oven. Add garlic and Prosciutto. Cook about 2 minutes, stirring constantly, until barely browned.
2. Add tomatoes and basil, and cover, leaving room for steam to escape so sauce will thicken. Let simmer 45 minutes.
3. Mix pasta into sauce. Serve hot, warm, or cold, as desired.

Serves 6.

Nutrient information per serving:

calories - 335; protein - 18 gm.; carbohydrate - 55 gm.; fat - 5 gm.; saturated fat - 1 gm.; percentage of calories from fat - 13; sodium - 923 mg.; cholesterol - 19 mg.; fiber - 5 gm.

ADA exchange value: 3 starch/bread, 2 vegetable, 2 lean meat

Fettuccine Alfredo

This is a basic Alfredo sauce that you can use as a springboard for your own culinary creativity. Spoon it over cooked chicken and top with sauteed mushrooms or sliced ripe olives. Add julienned vegetables for color and flavor and you have a primavera dish. Diced Canadian bacon and peas added to this sauce give you a carbonara sauce. So be creative and enjoy!

1 1/2 cups skim milk
1 Tbsp. Butter Buds®
2 Tbsp. cornstarch
1 cup light sour cream
freshly ground white or black pepper, to taste
3 oz. freshly grated Parmesan cheese
1 lb. fettuccine pasta, cooked al dente
Freshly chopped parsley to garnish

1. Mix milk, Butter Buds®, and cornstarch. Heat in a large saucepan until thick.
2. Mix in sour cream, pepper, and Parmesan cheese.
3. Toss sauce with pasta, garnish with parsley, and serve.

Serves 8.

Nutrient information per serving:

calories - 255; protein - 12 gm.; carbohydrate - 37 gm.; fat - 6 gm.; saturated fat - 2 gm.; percentage of calories from fat - 20; sodium - 240 mg.; cholesterol - 19 mg.; fiber - 1 gm.

ADA exchange value: 1 bread, 1 fat, 1/2 milk

SEAFOOD

Sole With Grapes

1 1/2 lbs. sole fillets
2 Tbsp. fresh lemon juice
3/4 cup dry white wine or dry vermouth
1 tsp. chervil
1/2 tsp. lemon peel
1/8 tsp. cayenne pepper (or to taste)
1 cup seedless green grapes, cut in half (about 30 grapes)
Paprika to garnish

1. In a skillet sprayed with a nonstick spray, heat and saute sole on each side. Transfer fish to a baking/serving dish.
2. Place remaining ingredients, except paprika, in skillet and heat.
3. Pour sauce over sole and bake at 350° until flaky (about 10 minutes).
4. Sprinkle with paprika and serve.

Serves 6.

Nutrient information per serving:

calories - 160; protein - 26 gm.; carbohydrate - 5 gm.; fat - 1 gm.; saturated fat - 0 gm.; percentage of calories from fat - 5; sodium - 92 mg.; cholesterol - 64 mg.; fiber - 0 gm.

ADA exchange value: 3 lean meat, 1/2 fruit

Shrimp Curry With Apples

Here's a meal that's a deal. Substitute chicken for the shrimp when you want a variation. Watch that curry powder—it can be powerful.

1 cup chicken stock
1/2 cup chopped onion
1/2 cup diced apple
1 clove garlic, minced
1/2 cup green pepper, chopped
2 cups low-fat yogurt
2 tsp. lemon juice
1/2 tsp. ground ginger
2 tsp. curry powder
1 dash chili powder
2 cups cooked shrimp
3 cups cooked brown rice

1. Heat a heavy nonstick skillet and add the chicken stock.
2. Saute onion, apple, and garlic. Cook until tender but not brown.
3. Add green pepper, yogurt, and all remaining ingredients. Cook on low heat, stirring constantly, until heated through.

NOTE: Don't boil this as the yogurt can curdle.

Serve over cooked rice.

Serves 6.

Nutrient information per serving:

calories - 224; protein - 16 gm.; carbohydrate - 33 gm.; fat - 2 gm.; saturated fat - 0 gm.; percentage of calories from fat - 9; sodium - 122 mg.; cholesterol - 64 mg.; fiber - 0 gm.

ADA exchange value: 2 lean meat, 1/2 fruit, 1 bread/starch

BBQ Swordfish

4 4-oz. swordfish fillets
1/2 cup low-sodium soy sauce
Juice from 1 lemon
1 Tbsp. grated ginger (1 tsp. dry)
1 clove garlic, chopped
1 tsp. dry mustard
1/4 tsp. cayenne pepper

1. Trim skin off swordfish. Rinse and pat dry.
2. Mix all other ingredients together in a dish or pan large enough to accommodate the swordfish.
3. Place swordfish in the marinade. Turn to cover both sides. Marinate 2 to 6 hours in the refrigerator, turning once.
4. Cook on a barbecue grill or broil until done to your likeness.

Serves 6.

Nutrient information per serving:

calories - 110; protein - 21 gm.; carbohydrate - 1 gm.; fat - 2 gm.; saturated fat - 0 gm.; percentage of calories from fat - 17; sodium - 396 mg.; cholesterol - 32 mg.; fiber - 0 gm.

ADA exchange value: 2 lean meat

Snapper With Spices

You can use any fish or shrimp with this recipe. I also like it with chicken.

4 6-oz. red snapper fillets
1 1/2 Tbsp. lemon juice
1 medium green bell pepper, thinly sliced
1 medium onion, thinly sliced
1/2 cup dry vermouth (or dry white wine)
1 Tbsp. freshly chopped parsley
1/2 tsp. dried basil
1/2 tsp. cayenne pepper
Freshly ground black pepper, to taste
1 14-oz. can diced tomatoes, drained
2 oz. freshly grated Parmesan cheese

1. Preheat oven to 350°.
2. Rinse and pat fish dry. Sprinkle fish with lemon juice.
3. In a skillet sprayed with olive oil, saute bell pepper and onion until soft.
4. Add vermouth, parsley, basil, cayenne pepper, and black pepper. Bring to a simmer. Remove from skillet. Turn heat to high, add fish, and cook 60 seconds on each side.
5. Transfer vegetable mixture and fish to a baking dish (either one large dish or four small ones). Top fish with tomatoes and sprinkle with Parmesan cheese.
6. Bake for 10 to 12 minutes and serve.

Serves 4.

Nutrient information per serving:

calories - 267; protein - 38 gm.; carbohydrate - 9 gm.; fat - 6 gm.; saturated fat - 3 gm.; percentage of calories from fat - 19; sodium - 565 mg.; cholesterol - 87 mg.; fiber - 2 gm.

ADA exchange value: 4 lean meat, 2 vegetable

Shrimp Scampi Provencal

30 medium shrimp, cleaned and peeled (approx. 1 lb.)
2 tsp. olive oil
1 clove garlic, minced
1 shallot, finely chopped
1/2 tsp. Italian herb blend (page 43)
2 celery stalks, very finely chopped
1/2 green bell pepper, finely chopped
1/2 red bell pepper, finely chopped
1 small carrot, finely chopped
1 lb. pasta
2 oz. fresh Parmesan cheese

1. Rinse shrimp and pat dry.
2. In nonstick skillet, heat olive oil. Add garlic and shallots and cook briefly.
3. Add Italian herb blend, celery, peppers, and carrots. Saute until soft.
4. Add shrimp and cook until just done.
5. Cook pasta until al dente. Toss with Parmesan cheese, top pasta with the shrimp and serve.

Serves 6.

Nutrient information per serving:

calories - 365; protein - 27 gm.; carbohydrate - 47 gm.; fat - 7 gm.; saturated fat - 2 gm.; percentage of calories from fat - 15; sodium - 316 mg.; cholesterol - 132 mg.; fiber - 2 gm.

ADA exchange value: 3 starch/bread, 3 lean meat

Scallops In White Wine

1 1/2 lbs. scallops
2 cups dry white wine or dry vermouth
4 shallots, chopped
2 lbs. mushrooms, chopped
2 Tbsp. freshly chopped parsley
1 tsp. herb salt blend (page 42)
1 lb. pasta
1/4 cup freshly grated Parmesan cheese

1. Wash scallops and pat dry. In large nonstick skillet, simmer scallops in wine for 5 minutes. Remove scallops and set aside.
2. Bring liquid to a boil. Add shallots and mushrooms. Cook until all liquid is absorbed. Then add scallops, parsley, and herb salt blend.
3. Cook pasta al dente. Drain and toss in Parmesan cheese.
4. Place scallop mixture on top and serve in pasta bowl.

Serves 6.

Nutrient information per serving:

calories - 401; protein - 28 gm.; carbohydrate - 54 gm.; fat - 3 gm.; saturated fat - 1 gm.; percentage of calories from fat - 8 ; sodium - 268 mg.; cholesterol - 42 mg.; fiber - 6 gm.

ADA exchange value: 2 starch/bread, 3 lean meat, 1 vegetable

Baked Halibut

4 halibut steaks, about 4.5 oz. each
1 lemon
1 tsp. herb salt blend (page 42)
1/2 lb. sliced mushrooms
1/2 cup dry vermouth

1. Trim skin off halibut, rinse, and pat dry.
2. Squeeze lemon on both sides of halibut.
3. Place halibut in a baking dish and sprinkle 1/4 tsp. herb salt over each steak.
4. Bake in oven preheated to 350° for 20 minutes (or until done).
5. Place mushrooms in nonstick skillet. Add vermouth, then cover and cook on medium heat for 5 minutes. Uncover and cook until all liquid is absorbed.
6. To serve, place mushrooms atop halibut.

Serves 4.

Nutrient information per serving:

calories - 236; protein - 39 gm.; carbohydrate - 3 gm.; fat - 4 gm.; saturated fat - 1 gm.; percentage of calories from fat - 16; sodium - 105 mg.; cholesterol - 60 mg.; fiber - 1 gm.

ADA exchange value: 4 lean meat, 1/2 vegetable

BAKED TROUT WITH LEMON HERBS

1 cup soft bread crumbs
3 Tbsp. grated Parmesan cheese
2 tsp. grated lemon rind
1 clove garlic, minced
1/2 tsp. dried whole thyme
1/2 tsp. dried whole basil
1/4 tsp. dried whole tarragon
1/4 tsp. pepper
3 Tbsp. chopped fresh parsley
6 trout fillets, 4 oz. each
1 1/2 Tbsp. reduced-calorie margarine, melted
1 Tbsp. lemon juice
Lemon twists to garnish

1. Combine first 8 ingredients in container of an electric blender and process until well blended.
2. Combine bread-crumb mixture and parsley and stir well.
3. Dredge fillets in bread-crumb mixture.
4. Arrange fillets in a single layer in a 13 x 9 x 2-inch baking dish coated with nonstick spray.
5. Combine melted margarine and lemon juice in a small bowl; drizzle over coated fillets.
6. Cover and bake at 500° for 10 minutes. Uncover and bake an additional 5 minutes or until fish flakes easily when tested with a fork.
7. Garnish with lemon twists and serve.

Serves 6.

Nutrient information per serving:

calories - 224; protein - 26 gm.; carbohydrate - 6 gm.; fat - 10.5 gm.; saturated fat - 3 gm.; percentage of calories from fat - 42; sodium - 182 mg.; cholesterol - 68 mg.; fiber - 0 gm.

ADA exchange value: 4 lean meat, 1 starch/bread

Shrimp-Stuffed Artichokes

4 artichokes, cooked
8 oz. cooked shrimp, cubed
2 celery stalks, diced
1/2 cup nonfat sour cream
1/4 cup low-calorie mayonnaise
1 Tbsp. dill weed
1/8 tsp. garlic powder
4-oz. can mandarin oranges
4 large red lettuce leaves

1. Remove the center core of the artichokes and scrape the remaining center leaves clean. Trim the points off the leaves and chill.
2. Mix shrimp, celery, sour cream, mayonnaise, dill weed, and garlic. Chill for 1 hour.
3. Fill artichokes with shrimp mixture and place on individual serving plates lined with red lettuce. Garnish with mandarin oranges, putting some oranges between the leaves of the artichokes.

Serves 4.

Nutrient information per serving:

calories - 230; protein - 17 gm.; carbohydrate - 20 gm.; fat - 9 gm.; saturated fat - 1 gm.; percentage of calories from fat - 34; sodium - 241 mg.; cholesterol - 113 mg.; fiber - 4 gm.

ADA exchange value: 2 lean meat, 1 vegetable, 1 fruit, 1 fat

Ginger-Orange Halibut

4 halibut steaks, about 5 oz. each
1 lemon, juiced
Freshly ground black pepper, to taste
2 tsp. cornstarch
1 tsp. freshly grated ginger
1/2 tsp. chicken bouillon powder
1 Tbsp. orange rind
1 Tbsp. soy sauce
1 green onion, finely chopped

1. Preheat broiler in oven.
2. Place halibut on broiler pan sprayed with nonstick spray, and sprinkle with lemon juice. Grind fresh pepper on top. Broil 4-inches from heat for 4 to 5 minutes. Turn fish over and sprinkle remaining lemon juice over the top. Grind fresh pepper on top and broil another 4 to 5 minutes.
3. While halibut is cooking, mix the remaining ingredients in a saucepan and heat until mixture thickens.
4. Pour sauce over halibut and serve.

Serves 4.

Nutrient information per serving:

calories - 209; protein - 38 gm.; carbohydrate - 2 gm.; fat - 4 gm.; saturated fat - 1 gm.; percentage of calories from fat - 17; sodium - 230 mg.; cholesterol - 60 mg.; fiber - 0 gm.

ADA exchange value: 4 lean meat

Poached Halibut and Peppers

4 halibut steaks (about 5 oz. each), skin removed
1 cup dry vermouth
1 bay leaf
1 red bell pepper, seeded, thinly sliced
1 green bell pepper, seeded, thinly sliced
1 yellow bell pepper, seeded, thinly sliced
1 medium onion, thinly sliced
2 celery stalks, thinly sliced
Paprika, cayenne pepper, and black pepper to taste

1. In a large skillet, bring vermouth with bay leaf to a boil. Add the halibut steaks and simmer until fish is done. Remove halibut and set aside. Discard bay leaf.
2. Bring liquid to a boil and reduce to 1/2 cup. Add remaining ingredients and simmer until all liquid is absorbed.
3. Serve vegetable mixture over halibut steaks.

Serves 4.

Nutrient information per serving:

calories - 268; protein - 39 gm.; carbohydrate - 6 gm.; fat - 4 gm.; saturated fat - 1 gm.; percentage of calories from fat - 14; sodium - 123 mg.; cholesterol - 60 mg.; fiber - 2 gm.

ADA exchange value: 4 lean meat

Spicy Shrimp

This is great served with plain rice and snow peas.

1 tsp. olive oil
1 lb. raw shrimp, cleaned and peeled
2 green onions, chopped
1 clove garlic, minced
2 Tbsp. fresh ginger, minced
2 Tbsp. sherry
2 Tbsp. soy sauce
4 Tbsp. ketchup
1/2 tsp. crushed red pepper (or to taste)

1. Heat oil in a wok. Add shrimp, onions, garlic, and ginger. Quickly stir-fry until shrimp is pink.
2. Add remaining ingredients and stir well.

Serves 4.

Nutrient information per serving:

calories - 198; protein - 27 gm.; carbohydrate - 8 gm.; fat - 4 gm.; saturated fat - 0 gm.; percentage of calories from fat - 16; sodium - 872 mg.; cholesterol - 200 mg.; fiber - 1 gm.

ADA exchange value: 3 lean meat

Fillet of Sole A La Bombay

This dish has the taste of India. Serve it with Indian Raisin Rice (p. 210).

1 1/2 lbs. fillet of sole
1/2 medium onion, sliced
1 cup dry white wine (or dry vermouth)
1 1/2 Tbsp. cornstarch
1/2 tsp. ground turmeric
1/4 tsp. ground ginger
1/4 tsp. ground cardamom
1/4 tsp. ground cumin
1/8 tsp. anise seed
1 cup nonfat sour cream
1/4 tsp. lemon peel

1. Rinse fish fillets and pat dry. Place in a large baking/serving dish.
2. In a skillet sprayed with olive oil, saute onions until soft. Add wine and remaining ingredients, mixing well.
3. Pour sauce over fish and bake in 350° oven until fish is done, about 20 to 30 minutes.

Serves 6.

Nutrient information per serving:

calories - 191; protein - 29 gm.; carbohydrate - 8 gm.; fat - 1 gm.; saturated fat - 0 gm.; percentage of calories from fat - 4; sodium - 144 mg.; cholesterol - 64 mg.; fiber - 0 gm.

ADA exchange value: 4 lean meat

Poached Whole Fish With Herbs

1 (4 lb.) whole bass
3 1/2 quarts water
1 cup sliced carrots
1 cup sliced celery
1 tsp. salt
6 peppercorns
1 bay leaf
1/8 tsp. thyme
1 tsp. lemon pepper

1. Thoroughly clean and scale fish. Wrap fish loosely in foil; do not seal.
2. In 5-quart saucepan, place foil-wrapped fish in the water and add remaining ingredients. Bring to a boil and reduce heat. Cook fish 15 minutes. Let stand in cooking liquid until ready to serve.

Serves 6.

Nutrient information per serving:

calories - 226; protein - 23 gm.; carbohydrate - 7 gm.; fat - 6.87 gm.; saturated fat - 1.5 gm.; percentage of calories from fat - 27; sodium - 533 mg.; cholesterol - 128 mg.; fiber - 0 gm.

ADA exchange value: 3 meat, 1 vegetable

Baked Cod

2 lbs. cod
1/2 cup sliced green onions
3/4 cup sliced celery
1 tsp. minced garlic
1 tomato, sliced
1/8 tsp. lemon pepper
3/4 tsp. dried thyme
1/2 tsp. dried basil
1/2 cup low-sodium tomato sauce

1. Preheat oven to 350°
2. In baking dish, layer onions, celery, garlic, and tomato slices.
3. Place cod on top of layer, and cover fish with a repeat layer.
4. Sprinkle with lemon pepper, thyme, and basil. Pour tomato sauce over top of fish.
5. Cover and bake for 25 minutes or until fish is done.

Serves 4.

Nutrient information per serving

calories - 211; protein - 31 gm.; carbohydrate - 9 gm.; fat - 1.3 gm.; saturated fat - 0.26 gm.; percentage of calories from fat - .05; sodium - 176 mg.; cholesterol - 82 mg.; fiber - 0 gm.

ADA exchange value: 6 meat

Dilly Lemon Fish Fillets

1 pkg. (11 1/2 oz.) frozen fish, thawed
2 Tbsp. lemon juice
1/8 tsp. salt
1/8 tsp. lemon pepper
1/8 tsp. paprika
2 Tbsp. light mayonnaise
2 Tbsp. plain low-fat yogurt
1 tsp. dried dillweed
1 tomato, sliced
1/2 tsp. dried parsley flakes, crushed

1. Preheat oven to 450°.
2. Place fish in a shallow baking dish.
3. Brush fish with lemon juice; sprinkle with salt, lemon pepper, and paprika.
4. Bake for 10 minutes or until fish flakes easily.
5. Meanwhile, stir together mayonnaise, yogurt, dillweed, and parsley. Spoon over fish. Serve with tomatoes.

Serves 4.

Nutrient information per serving:

calories - 168; protein - 29 gm.; carbohydrate - 7 gm.; fat - 11.2 gm.; saturated fat - 0.25 gm.; percentage of calories from fat - 6; sodium - 271 mg.; cholesterol - 1.2 mg.; fiber - 0 gm.

ADA exchange value: 2 lean meat, 1 fat

Fish Italian

1 Tbsp. vegetable oil
1 cup chopped onions
1/4 cup green onions, sliced
2 lbs. haddock fillets
1 cup diced tomatoes
1 tsp. dried parsley flakes, crushed
1/8 tsp. pepper
1/2 tsp. garlic powder
3 Tbsp. dry white wine
1 tsp. Italian herb blend (page 43)

1. Heat oil in a skillet. Add all onions Saute for 3 to 4 minutes.
2. Place onions in an 8-inch square baking dish.
3. Cut fish fillets into 6 portions and place atop the onions. Season fish with pepper and garlic powder. Place tomatoes on top of fish; sprinkle with Italian herbs, parsley flakes, and wine. Cover and bake in preheated 375° oven for 20 minutes.

Serves 6.

Nutrient information per serving:

calories - 216; protein - 41 gm.; carbohydrate - 9 gm.; fat - 5.86 gm.; saturated fat - 0.86 gm.; percentage of calories from fat - 24; sodium - 86 mg.; cholesterol - 47.7 mg.; fiber - 0 gm.

ADA exchange value: 4 meat, 1 vegetable, 1/2 fat

Broiled Halibut 'N' Herbs

1 lb. halibut
1/2 cup lemon juice
3/4 cup water
1/4 cup skim milk
1 Tbsp. flour
1/2 tsp. dried tarragon
1 tsp. minced onion
1/8 tsp. basil
1/8 tsp. black pepper
1/2 tsp. sage
1/8 tsp. Tabasco sauce

1. Marinate fish in lemon juice for about 1 hour.
2. Broil fish until done; keep fish warm.
3. In saucepan, combine water, milk, and flour, stirring until smooth. Cook over low heat until slightly thickened. Add seasonings and cook 5 minutes longer.
4. Pour sauce over fish portions and serve.

Serves 4.

Nutrient information per serving

calories - 150; protein - 40 gm.; carbohydrate - 11 gm.; fat - 2.7 gm.; saturated fat - 0.4 gm.; percentage of calories from fat - 16; sodium - 70 mg.; cholesterol - 37.6 mg.; fiber - 0

ADA exchange value: 3 meat

Fish with Five Spices

2 lbs. halibut fillets
2/3 cup green onions, chopped
1 1/2 Tbsp. fresh ginger, crushed
1/2 cup soy sauce
1 1/2 Tbsp. sugar
1 Tbsp. sesame oil
1/2 tsp. ground cinnamon
1/2 tsp. allspice
1/4 tsp. ground cloves
1/8 tsp. anise seed

1. Cut fish in 2-inch squares.
2. Mix fish with onions, ginger, soy sauce, sugar, oil, and spices. Cover and chill for several hours.
3. Broil on both sides until fish is opaque.

Serves 8.

Nutrient information per serving:

calories - 158; protein - 41 gm.; carbohydrate - 9 gm.; fat - 4.42 gm.; saturated fat - 0.237 gm.; percentage of calories from fat - 25; sodium - 886.6 mg.; cholesterol - 0 mg.; fiber - 0 gm.

ADA exchange value: 3 meat

Baked Sea Perch

1 lb. sea perch
1/3 cup white wine
1/4 cup sliced onion
1/4 cup sliced green onion
1/8 tsp. lemon pepper
1 tsp. minced garlic
1/8 tsp. dried tarragon
1/2 tsp. dried thyme
1/4 tsp. basil
1 tomato, sliced

1. Place all ingredients into a bowl and marinate for 1 hour.
2. Place fish and marinade into a baking dish and bake for 25 minutes at 350°F.

Serves 3.

Nutrient information per serving:

calories - 184; protein - 31 gm.; carbohydrate - 8 gm.; fat - 1.4 gm.; saturated fat - 0.35 gm.; percentage of calories from fat - .06; sodium - 98 mg.; cholesterol - 141 mg.; fiber - 0 gm.

ADA exchange value: 3 meat

Baked Shrimp

12 raw jumbo shrimp, shelled and deveined
1/2 cup melted margarine
1 cup dry bread crumbs
1 tsp. dried parsley flakes
1 Tbsp. fresh dill, finely chopped
1/4 cup dry white wine
1/8 tsp. pepper
1 tsp. celery seed

1. Preheat oven to 350°.
2. With a sharp knife, split shrimp in half lengthwise along the inside curve, being careful not to cut all the way through; set aside.
3. Combine margarine and remaining ingredients.
4. Stuff each shrimp with about 2 Tbsp of the mixture.
5. Place in baking dish. Bake at 350° for 20 minutes.

Serves 6.

Nutrient information per serving:

calories - 235; protein - 27 gm.; carbohydrate - 9 gm.; fat - 8.8 gm.; saturated fat - 1.3 gm.; percentage of calories from fat - 34; sodium - 215 mg.; cholesterol - 130 mg.; fiber - 0 gm.

ADA exchange value: 3 meat, 1 1/2 fat, 1 starch/bread

Broiled Fish With Tomatoes Vinaigrette

2 Tbsp. vegetable oil
1 Tbsp. vinegar
1 1/2 tsp. ground coriander
3/4 tsp. minced garlic
1/2 tsp. dried parsley flakes
1/2 tsp. tarragon
1 tsp. oregano
2 cups coarsely chopped tomatoes
4 trout fillets

1. Beat together oil, vinegar, coriander, and garlic. Add parsley, tarragon and oregano, and mix. Stir in tomatoes.
2. Place fish on broiler pan and brush lightly with oil. Broil fish until done.
3. Pour dressing over fish and serve.

Serves 4.

Nutrient information per serving:

calories - 178; protein - 27 gm.; carbohydrate - 8 gm.; fat - 7 gm.; saturated fat - 0.9 gm.; percentage of calories from fat - 35; sodium - 8.7 mg. cholesterol - 48 mg.; fiber - 0 gm.

ADA exchange value: 2 meat, 1 fat

Tuna Casserole

1 cup noodles
1 cup skim milk
1 Tbsp. flour
1 6 1/8-oz. can tuna in spring water, drained
3/4 cup fresh mushrooms, sliced
1 Tbsp. minced onion
1/4 cup finely chopped red pepper
1 tsp. dried parsley flakes
1 tsp. basil
1 tsp. celery seed
1/8 tsp. black pepper

1. Cook noodles in water until done; drain.
2. In saucepan, add milk and flour; cook until thickened.
3. In bowl, combine tuna, mushrooms, onions, red pepper, and seasonings; mix well. Add milk mixture; mix again. Stir in noodles.
4. In baking dish bake at 325° for 40 minutes.

Serves 4.

Nutrient information per serving:

calories - 289; protein - 28 gm.; carbohydrate - 33 gm.; fat - 6.3 gm.; saturated fat - 0.05 gm.; percentage of calories from fat - 20; sodium - 114 mg.; cholesterol - 83 mg.; fiber - 2 gm.

ADA exchange value: 1 1/2 meat, 1 1/2 starch/bread, 1 vegetable

Tuna Souffle

2 6 1/8-oz. cans tuna in spring water
1/2 cup bran cereal, uncooked
1/2 cup skim milk
2 Tbsp. minced onion
1 Tbsp. lime juice
1 Tbsp. dried parsley flakes
1/8 tsp. black pepper
1 tsp. celery seed
1/8 tsp. paprika
1 egg white

1. Heat oven to 325°.
2. Drain tuna and flake. In a large bowl, mix tuna, bran, milk, onion, lime juice, parsley, pepper, celery seed, and paprika.
3. Beat egg white until stiff peak forms; fold into tuna mixture. Put into a 1-quart baking dish. Bake for 40 minutes or until brown.

Serves 6.

Nutrient information per serving:

calories - 139; protein - 41 gm.; carbohydrate - 38 gm.; fat - 1.3 gm.; saturated fat - 0.31 gm.; percentage of calories from fat - 0; sodium - 40 mg.; cholesterol - 426 mg.; fiber - 0 gm.

ADA exchange value: 1 meat, 1 starch/bread

Provencal Fish

2 tsp. oil
2/3 cup onions, chopped
1 tsp. minced garlic
1 cup chopped tomatoes
3/4 tsp. dried basil
1/4 tsp. oregano
1 tsp. dried parsley flakes
1 1/2 Tbsp. lemon juice
8 oz. walleye fillet
1/8 tsp. pepper
1/8 tsp. salt
1/4 cup water

1. Heat oil in a skillet. Add onion and garlic, and saute until golden.
2. Stir in tomatoes, basil, oregano, parsley, and lemon juice.
3. Sprinkle fish with salt and pepper. Lay fish on top of sauce in skillet and add water. Cover and steam fish for 10 minutes or until fish flakes easily.

Serves 2.

Nutrient information per serving

calories - 191; protein - 18 gm.; carbohydrate - 7 gm.; fat - 5.8 gm.; saturated fat - 0.8 gm.; percentage of calories from fat - 27; sodium - 210 mg.; cholesterol - 97 mg.; fiber - 0 gm.

ADA exchange value: 3 meat, 1 vegetable, 1 fat

POULTRY

BBQ Chicken With Herb Vinegar And Basil

4 whole chicken legs, skinned
3/4 cup low-salt chicken broth
2 Tbsp. herb vinegar
1/2 cup dry vermouth
2 shallots, chopped
1 tsp. mace
1/4 tsp. freshly ground black pepper
2 tsp. dried basil

1. Rinse and pat chicken dry.
2. Bring remaining ingredients to a simmer in a skillet large enough to hold the chicken.
3. Add the chicken to sauce, cover, and simmer 20 minutes, turning once.
4. Remove from heat and refrigerate for 4 to 8 hours (or overnight).
5. Cook chicken on a barbecue until done. This recipe can also be cooked in the broiler, about 8 minutes on each side.
6. Either discard the marinade or bring it to a boil if you wish to pour it over the chicken.

Serves 4.

Nutrient information per serving:

calories - 118; protein - 17 gm.; carbohydrate - 1 gm.; fat - 2 gm.; saturated fat - 1 gm.; percentage of calories from fat - 17; sodium - 83 mg.; cholesterol - 44 mg.; fiber - 0 gm.

ADA exchange value: 2 lean meat

Chicken Thighs With An Indian Flair

Serve this with Indian Raisin Rice (page 210.)

8 chicken thighs, skinned, fat removed
1 cup nonfat plain yogurt
2 Tbsp. fresh lemon juice
2 tsp. freshly grated ginger
2 cloves garlic, minced
1 tsp. ground cumin
1 tsp. turmeric
1/2 tsp. cayenne pepper
1 tsp. cornstarch, mixed with 2 Tbsp. cold water

1. Rinse chicken thighs and pat dry.
2. Mix remaining ingredients, except cornstarch. Place thighs in yogurt mixture and marinate in refrigerator, covered, for 8 hours.
3. Place thighs in a baking pan sprayed with nonstick spray and bake in preheated oven at 350° for 15 minutes.
4. Place the marinade in a sauce pan and bring to simmer. Add the cornstarch mixture, stirring until slightly thickened.
5. Pour the marinade over the chicken thighs and bake for 15 minutes more. Then serve.

Serves 4.

Nutrient information per serving:

calories - 221; protein - 36 gm.; carbohydrate - 6 gm.; fat - 4 gm.; saturated fat - 1 gm.; percentage of calories from fat - 9; sodium - 103 mg.; cholesterol - 88 mg.; fiber - 0 gm.

ADA exchange value: 4 lean meat

Chicken In Lettuce Cups

This dish is great as finger food, for picnics, and on warm summer nights.

1 1/2 lb. chicken breast, chopped fine
1 Tbsp. cornstarch
3 Tbsp. dry sherry
2 cloves garlic, chopped
8 oz. mushrooms, chopped
1 Tbsp. freshly chopped ginger
1 Tbsp. dark sesame oil
1/2 cup water chestnuts, chopped
1/2 tsp. freshly ground black pepper
3 Tbsp. low-sodium soy sauce
12 lettuce cups (iceberg or bibb)

1. Combine cornstarch and sherry and mix into chicken. Cover and put in refrigerator to marinate for 15 minutes.
2. In large wok or skillet sprayed with olive oil, saute garlic and scallions lightly. Add mushrooms and 1 Tbsp. water. Stir and cover for 3 minutes. Remove cover and cook until all water is gone. Add ginger, then remove from pan and set aside.
3. Heat sesame oil in wok or skillet, add chicken, and cook quickly, using a stir-fry method.
4. Add mushroom mixture, water chestnuts, pepper, soy sauce, and mix well.
5. Divide the mixture into the 12 lettuce cups and serve.

Serves 6.

Nutrient information per serving:

calories - 245; protein - 10 gm.; carbohydrate -45 gm.; fat - 3 gm.; saturated fat - 1 gm.; percentage of calories from fat - 11; sodium - 385 mg.; cholesterol - 6 mg.; fiber - 5 gm.

ADA exchange value: 3 lean meat, 1 vegetable

Chicken Polynesian

4 chicken breasts, boned and skinned
1/4 cup low-sodium soy sauce
1 tsp. ginger
1 tsp. onion powder
1/2 cup all-purpose flour
4 oz. canned pineapple chunks
4 oz. canned mandarin oranges
2 Tbsp. cornstarch
1/4 cup water
1/4 cup toasted almonds

1. Rinse and pat chicken dry. Place in shallow pan.
2. Combine soy sauce, ginger, and onion powder, and pour over chicken. Cover and marinate in refrigerator one to two hours.
3. Put flour in a bag, add chicken, and shake chicken breasts until they are well coated. Spray a large nonstick skillet with nonstick spray, heat pan, and brown chicken on both sides. Return chicken back to baking pan.
4. Add juice of pineapple and oranges to the marinade mixture and pour it into skillet.
5. Combine cornstarch and water and pour mixture into skillet. Stir over heat until sauce is thickened. Pour sauce over chicken and bake 20 minutes at 350°.
6. Add fruit and almonds to chicken dish and bake 10 minutes more.

Serves 4.

Nutrient information per serving:

calories - 353; protein - 37 gm.; carbohydrate - 30 gm.; fat - 9 gm.; saturated fat - 2 gm.; percentage of calories from fat - 23; sodium - 1107 mg.; cholesterol - 88 mg.; fiber - 2 gm.

ADA exchange value: 1 starch/bread, 5 lean meat, 1 fruit

Chicken Cacciatore

Serve this with the pasta of your choice.

6 chicken legs and thighs, skin removed
1 onion, sliced
1 green bell pepper, sliced
16 oz. mushrooms, sliced
1/4 cup red wine (or dry vermouth)
1 28-oz. can tomato paste
1 tsp. Italian seasoning blend (page 43)
1/2 tsp. basil
1/2 tsp. crushed red pepper
1 Tbsp. freshly chopped parsley
1 oz. freshly grated Parmesan cheese
1 lb. pasta, cooked al dente

1. In a large cast-iron pot, or Dutch oven sprayed with olive oil, brown the chicken on both sides. Then remove chicken from pot.
2. Add onion and green peppers to pot and cook until soft. Remove these from pot.
3. Add mushrooms and wine to pot, cover and simmer for 2 minutes. Uncover and cook until most of the liquid is absorbed.
4. Add tomatoes, tomato paste, Italian seasoning, basil, and crushed red pepper. Bring to a boil, then reduce heat to simmer.
5. Add chicken to sauce and cover, leaving an opening for steam to escape. Simmer for 45 minutes.
6. Remove chicken; add parsley and Parmesan cheese to sauce.
7. Place hot pasta in a large pasta bowl and cover with sauce. Top with chicken.

Serves 6.

Nutrient information per serving:

calories - 490; protein - 45 gm.; carbohydrate - 59 gm.; fat - 8 gm.; saturated fat - 2 gm.; percentage of calories from fat - 14; sodium - 304 mg.; cholesterol - 92 mg.; fiber - 6 gm.

ADA exchange value: 3 starch/bread, 4 lean meat, 2 vegetable

Chicken Chili With Veggies

This recipe is ideal for using either leftover chicken or turkey. It takes a little longer to prepare, but it's well worth it. Plus you can freeze this one for later use.

1/2 cup chopped green bell pepper
1/4 cup chopped onion
2 cloves garlic, chopped fine
2 tsp. olive oil
3 cups cut-up cooked chicken or turkey
1/2 cup water
1 Tbsp. snipped fresh oregano leaves (1 tsp. dried)
1 Tbsp. chili powder
1 tsp. ground cumin
1/2 tsp. salt
1 16-oz. can whole tomatoes, undrained
1 10-oz. pkg. frozen mixed vegetables
2 cups zucchini slices (cut to about 1/2 inch)

1. In a 3-quart saucepan, cook and stir bell pepper, onion, and garlic in oil over medium heat until the onion is tender.
2. Stir in remaining ingredients except frozen vegetables and zucchini. Break up the tomatoes.
3. Heat mixture to boiling. Reduce heat, cover, and simmer for one hour, stirring occasionally.
4. Add the frozen vegetables and zucchini. Heat to boiling again, reduce heat, then simmer uncovered, stirring occasionally, until zucchini is crisp-tender.

Makes six 1-cup servings.

Nutrient information per serving:

calories - 200; protein - 24 gm.; carbohydrate - 13 gm.; fat - 6 gm.; saturated fat - 1 gm.; percentage of calories from fat - 27; sodium - 510 mg.; cholesterol - 55 mg.; fiber - 6 gm.

ADA exchange value: 4 lean meat, 2 vegetable

Turkey Sausage

Who says you can't enjoy sausage. This has all the flavor of sausage with very little fat.

1 lb. ground turkey (mixture of dark and light meat)
1/2 tsp. marjoram
1/2 tsp. sage
1/2 tsp. crushed red pepper
1/2 tsp. ground black pepper
1/2 tsp. light salt

1. Place all ingredients in food processor with steel blade and process until well mixed.
2. Make 12 patties and fry until well done in nonstick skillet sprayed with nonstick spray. You can also freeze the patties and use them in other recipes.

Serves 6.

Nutrient information per serving:

calories - 96; protein - 18 gm.; carbohydrate - 0 gm.; fat - 2 gm.; saturated fat - 1 gm.; percentage of calories from fat - 18; sodium - 221 mg.; cholesterol - 43 mg.; fiber - 0 gm.

ADA exchange value: 2 lean meat

Turkey Sausage With Peppers And Onions

Serve with pasta or rice.

1 lb. turkey sausage made into 12 patties (from recipe on page 138).
2 medium onions, sliced
2 green bell peppers, seeded and sliced
1 28-oz. can diced tomatoes in juice
1/2 tsp. crushed red pepper
1/2 tsp. Italian seasoning

1. In a large nonstick skillet sprayed with nonstick spray, brown the turkey patties on both sides. Remove from skillet and set aside.
2. Add onions and bell pepper to skillet and saute until soft. Add tomatoes and seasonings. Simmer 15 minutes.
3. Add sausage patties to skillet and cover them with sauce. Cover and simmer 15 minutes.

Serves 6.

Nutrient information per serving:

calories - 128; protein - 19 gm.; carbohydrate - 7 gm.; fat - 2 gm.; saturated fat - 1 gm.; percentage of calories from fat - 16; sodium - 337 mg.; cholesterol - 43 mg.; fiber - 2 gm.

ADA exchange value: 2 lean meat, 1 vegetable

Country Sausage Gravy

I grew up with homemade biscuits and gravy. Here is a version that is low in fat and tastes great over biscuits or rice.

1/2 lb. turkey sausage (from recipe on page 138)
3 Tbsp. flour
2 cups 1% milk
freshly ground black pepper to taste

1. In nonstick skillet sprayed with nonstick spray, break up sausage and brown well.
2. Mix flour, milk, and pepper. Pour into skillet with sausage. Bring mixture to a boil, stirring constantly until thick.

Serves 4.

Nutrient information per serving:

calories - 143; protein - 18 gm.; carbohydrate - 10 gm.; fat - 3 gm.; saturated fat - 1 gm.; percentage of calories from fat - 18; sodium - 228 mg.; cholesterol - 37 mg.; fiber - 0 gm.

ADA exchange value: 1/2 starch/bread, 2 lean meat

Orange-Rosemary Cornish Game Hens

2 Cornish game hens, rinsed inside and out, patted dry
2 cloves garlic, peeled
1 orange, quartered
4 sprigs fresh rosemary (or 1 Tbsp. dry)
2 Tbsp. sugar-free orange marmalade
1 Tbsp. rosemary chopped (or 1 1/2 tsp. dry)

1. Preheat oven to 350°.
2. In each hen, place 1 clove garlic, 2 quarters of the orange, and 2 sprigs of rosemary.
3. Place hens in roasting pan and roast for 70 minutes.
4. Mix orange marmalade and chopped rosemary and baste hens. Roast 10 minutes longer.

Serves 4.

Nutrient information per serving:

calories - 200; protein - 28 gm.; carbohydrate - 11 gm.; fat - 4 gm.; saturated fat - 1 gm.; percentage of calories from fat - 20; sodium - 78 mg.; cholesterol - 101 mg.; fiber - 1 gm.

ADA exchange value: 3 lean meat, 1/2 fruit

Cornish Hens With Roasted Spices

Here's another variation for using succulent Cornish game hens. In this recipe the hens are blackened to create an entirely new taste and texture. Even though the preparation time is longer than 15 minutes, this dish is well worth the effort. There's a surprise in here: espresso.

2 Tbsp. sesame seeds
1/4 tsp. coriander seeds
1/4 tsp. black peppercorns
3 whole cloves
1 stick cinnamon (about 1/4 inch)
1/4 bay leave
1 Tbsp. freshly ground espresso beans
1 tsp. sugar
1/4 tsp. salt
3 Cornish game hens (about 1 lb. each), skin removed
2 tsp. olive oil
Fresh coriander sprigs for garnish

1. Place the first six ingredients into small piles on a baking sheet and bake in a 300° oven for 25 minutes, just until the sesame seeds are golden in color.
2. Set 1 Tbsp. roasted sesame seeds aside.
3. Combine the remaining spices and, using your mortar and pestle, crush them until they are totally pulverized.
4. Move the spice mixture into a small bowl; add the ground espresso, sugar, and salt. Mix well and set aside.
5. Remove giblets from hens and rinse the hens under cold, running water. Pat hens dry and split each in half lengthwise.
6. Rub the spice mixture over the entire surface of the hens and place the hens in a 2-inch deep baking dish. Cover the dish and marinate the birds for 8 hours.

7. Spray a large nonstick skillet with cooking spray.
8. Add the olive oil and heat over medium-high heat until the oil is hot. Add the hens, skin-side down. Saute 5 minutes. Turn hens and reduce heat to medium. Cover and cook 20 to 30 minutes or until hens are done.
9. Sprinkle with reserved roasted sesame seeds and garnish with fresh coriander sprigs.

Serves 6.

Nutrient information per serving:

calories - 183; protein - 26.7 gm.; carbohydrate - 1.5 gm.; fat - 7.1 gm.; saturated fat - 2 gm.; percentage of calories from fat - 34; sodium - 193 mg.; cholesterol - 84 mg.; fiber - 1 gm.

ADA exchange value: 3 lean meat

Orange and Onion Chicken

6 chicken breast halves with bone, skinned
2 Tbsp. flour
1/2 tsp. herb salt (page 42)
1/4 tsp. freshly ground black pepper
2 onions, thinly sliced
Zest of one thinly sliced orange
1 cup orange juice
2 tsp. fresh thyme (1/2 tsp. dried)
2 Tbsp. fresh lemon juice
1 Tbsp. sugar
3/4 cup dry white wine or dry vermouth

1. Rinse chicken breast and pat dry. Put flour, herb salt, and pepper in a bag and shake chicken to coat.
2. In skillet sprayed with olive oil, brown chicken breast on meat side. Remove chicken from pan and place in baking pan that has been sprayed with a nonstick spray.
3. Deglaze pan with 1/4 cup of the wine. Add onion and cook until soft.
4. Add orange zest, orange juice, thyme, lemon juice, sugar, and remaining wine and bring to a boil. Reduce to half.
5. Pour over chicken and bake uncovered in a preheated oven at 350° for 45 minutes or until chicken is done.

Serves 6.

Nutrient information per serving:

calories - 248; protein - 34 gm.; carbohydrate - 11 gm.; fat - 5 gm.; saturated fat - 1 gm.; percentage of calories from fat - 16; sodium - 120 mg.; cholesterol - 88 mg.; fiber - 1 gm.

ADA exchange value: 4 lean meat, 1/2 fruit

Chicken Stew (The Easy Way)

Here is a pleasant stew to serve with whole wheat bread and a tossed green salad. This great-tasting stew can be made in your crock pot, cooked on low for 8 hours.

1 1/2 lb. chicken thighs, skinned
2 10-oz. pkgs. of frozen stew vegetables
1 can low-fat, low-salt tomato soup
1 1/2 tsp. chicken herb blend

1. Preheat oven to 300°.
2. In a casserole, mix all ingredients, cover, and bake for 3 hours.

Serves 6.

Nutrient information per serving:

calories - 261; protein - 26 gm.; carbohydrate - 30 gm.; fat - 3 gm.; saturated fat - 1 gm.; percentage of calories from fat - 10; sodium - 467 mg.; cholesterol - 59 mg.; fiber - 0 gm.

ADA exchange value: 3 lean meat, 3 vegetable

Cilantro Chicken Breast

4 chicken breast halves, boned and skinned (4 oz. each)
2 shallots, chopped
4 sun-dried tomatoes, diced
1 cup low-sodium chicken broth
1 Tbsp. cornstarch mixed with 1/2 cup cold water
1/2 tsp. freshly ground black pepper
1/2 cup light sour cream
1/2 cup fresh cilantro, chopped

1. In a large skillet sprayed with olive oil, brown chicken breast on both sides. Add shallots, tomatoes, and chicken broth; cover and simmer for 20 minutes (until chicken is done). Remove chicken from pan and keep warm.
2. Add cornstarch mixture to broth and stir until thickened. Add pepper, sour cream, and cilantro, mix.
3. Pour sauce over chicken and serve.

Serves 4.

Nutrient information per serving:

calories - 202; protein - 27 gm.; carbohydrate - 9 gm.; fat - 5 gm.; saturated fat - 1 gm.; percentage of calories from fat - 22; sodium - 142 mg.; cholesterol - 76 mg.; fiber - 2 gm.

ADA exchange value: 3 lean meat, 1 vegetable

Oven-Fried Herbed Chicken

4 chicken breast halves, boned and skinned, pounded to 1/2 inch
1/2 tsp. freshly ground black pepper
Pinch salt
3 Tbsp. Dijon mustard
1/2 cup nonfat plain yogurt
1/2 tsp. caraway seeds
2 tsp. dried chervil
3 Tbsp. freshly chopped parsley
1 cup dried bread crumbs

1. Rinse and pat chicken dry.
2. Mix pepper, salt, mustard, yogurt, caraway seeds, chervil, and parsley.
3. Coat the chicken on both sides with the mixture and then dip chicken in bread crumbs.
4. Place chicken on baking sheet lined with foil and sprayed with olive oil. Spray each chicken breast lightly with the olive oil spray.
5. Bake in a preheated oven at 500° for 30 minutes.

Serves 4.

Nutrient information per serving:

calories - 260; protein - 30 gm.; carbohydrate - 21 gm.; fat - 5 gm.; saturated fat - 1 gm.; percentage of calories from fat - 17; sodium - 466 mg.; cholesterol - 67 mg.; fiber - 1 gm.

ADA exchange value: 1 starch/bread, 4 lean meat

Cajun Chicken

8 chicken thighs, skin and fat removed
1/2 tsp. caraway seed
1/2 tsp. cayenne pepper
3/4 tsp. ground coriander
3/4 tsp. ground cumin
3 cloves garlic, minced
1 1/2 tsp. dry mustard
1/4 tsp. thyme
1/4 cup cognac
2 Tbsp. fresh lemon juice

1. Rinse and pat chicken dry.
2. Place all ingredients, except chicken, in a mini chopper and pulverize.
3. Line a baking sheet with foil. Coat each piece of chicken with spice mixture, and place on baking sheet. Bake in oven preheated to 350° for 35 to 45 minutes.

Serves 4.

Nutrient information per serving:

calories - 209; protein - 33 gm.; carbohydrate - 2 gm.; fat - 3 gm.; saturated fat - 1 gm.; percentage of calories from fat - 19; sodium - 75 mg.; cholesterol - 88 mg.; fiber - 0 gm.

ADA exchange value: 4 lean meat

Rolled Chicken With Asparagus

This makes an excellent dish to serve company.

3 chicken breasts, boned, halved, skinned, and pounded
18 medium asparagus spears, bottoms trimmed, blanched
1 small clove garlic, minced
1/4 cup Dijon mustard
1/4 cup dry vermouth
1 cup bread crumbs
1 Tbsp. grated Parmesan cheese
1 tsp. Italian blend (page 43)
2 Tbsp. freshly chopped parsley

1. Preheat oven to 350°.
2. Mix mustard, garlic, and vermouth.
3. Coat both sides of chicken breast with mixture. Roll chicken around 3 asparagus spears, and secure with toothpick.
4. Mix bread crumbs, Parmesan cheese, Italian blend, and parsley together. Roll chicken rolls in mixture.
5. Place chicken in baking dish sprayed with olive oil. Lightly spray the tops of the chicken rolls with olive oil and bake for 30 minutes.

Serves 6.

Nutrient information per serving:

calories - 93; protein - 10 gm.; carbohydrate - 8 gm.; fat - 2 gm.; saturated fat - 0 gm.; percentage of calories from fat - 17; sodium - 154 mg.; cholesterol - 23 mg.; fiber - 1 gm.

ADA exchange value: 1 starch/bread, 3 lean meat

Chicken Chasseur

This is good served with brown or white rice and a green vegetable.

6 chicken breasts, halved, boned, and skin removed
8 oz. mushrooms, sliced
1/2 cup dry white wine or dry vermouth
1 medium onion, sliced
1 28-oz. can whole tomatoes (pureed in blender)
2 tsp. tarragon
2 tsp. chervil
1/2 tsp. ground black pepper
Freshly chopped parsley for garnish

1. Spray a large skillet with olive oil spray. Heat skillet and brown chicken breasts on both sides, then remove from pan.
2. Add mushrooms to pan along with 1/4 cup wine. Cover and simmer for 2 minutes. Remove cover, turn up heat, and cook until all liquid is absorbed. Remove mushrooms from pan.
3. Add onion to pan and saute until soft. Add remaining wine.
4. Return mushrooms to the pan and add tomatoes, tarragon, chervil, and pepper. Bring to a boil, then reduce heat to simmer.
5. Place chicken in the pan, covering so steam can escape to reduce the sauce. Simmer for 30 minutes.

Serves 6.

Nutrient information per serving:

calories - 282; protein - 43 gm.; carbohydrate - 9 gm.; fat - 6 gm.; saturated fat - 2 gm.; percentage of calories from fat - 19; sodium - 480 mg.; cholesterol - 110 mg.; fiber - 3 gm.

ADA exchange value: 5 lean meat, 2 vegetable

Basil Chicken

2 boneless, skinned chicken breasts, halved
1/4 cup low-sodium soy sauce
1/2 tsp. garlic powder
1 tsp. dried basil

1. Baste chicken with soy sauce.
2. Sprinkle chicken with garlic powder and basil.
3. Broil chicken. basting with soy sauce as chicken broils.

Serves 4.

Nutrient information per serving:

calories - 173; protein - 33 gm.; carbohydrate - 2 gm.; fat - 5.3 gm.; saturated fat - 1.7 gm.; percentage of calories from fat - 28; sodium - 825 mg.; cholesterol - 73 mg.; fiber - 0 gm.

ADA exchange value: 1 1/2 lean meat

Chicken Bake

2 chicken breasts, skinless, boneless
1 1/2 cups low-sodium chicken broth
1 1/2 Tbsp. lime juice
1/2 tsp. crushed basil
1/2 tsp. crushed oregano
1/8 tsp. celery seed
1/2 tsp. lime rind, grated

1. Preheat oven to 325°.
2. Place chicken in shallow baking dish.
3. Combine broth, lime juice, basil, oregano, celery seed, and lime rind; pour over the chicken.
4. Cover and bake for 45 to 50 minutes.

Serves 2.

Nutrient information per serving:

calories - 230; protein - 24 gm.; carbohydrate - 15 gm.; fat - 5.3 gm.; saturated fat - 1.4 gm.; percentage of calories from fat - 21; sodium - 78 mg.; cholesterol - 61 mg.; fiber - 0 gm.

ADA exchange value: 3 lean meat

Chicken And Vegetables From The Skillet

10-oz. pkg. frozen Brussels sprouts, thawed
2 whole chicken breasts, skinned and cut into strips
Dash salt
Dash pepper
1 Tbsp. vegetable oil
1/2 cup chopped onion
1 1/2 tsp. lemon juice
3/4 tsp. crushed basil
2 cups tomatoes, coarsely chopped

1. Put Brussels sprouts in a colander and run hot water over them; drain and halve. Set aside.
2. Season chicken with salt and pepper.
3. In a skillet, heat oil and cook chicken strips and onion on medium-high heat until done. Stir in Brussels sprouts, lemon juice, and basil. Reduce heat and cook for 10 minutes. Stir in tomatoes. Cook for 2 minutes more.

Serves 4.

Nutrient information per serving:

calories - 164; protein - 23 gm.; carbohydrate - 28 gm.; fat - 5.75 gm.; saturated fat - 1.15 gm.; percentage of calories from fat - 32; sodium - 123 mg.; cholesterol - 43 mg.; fiber - 1 gm.

ADA exchange value: 2 lean meat, 1 vegetable

Chicken Breast Cacciatore

1 Tbsp. vegetable oil
1 Tbsp. minced garlic
3 chicken breasts, skinned and cut in halves
3/4 cup chopped onion
3/4 cup chopped green pepper
1 cup fresh tomatoes, peeled and chopped
1/4 tsp. basil
1/8 tsp. pepper
1/4 tsp. rosemary
1/4 cup dry white wine

1. Heat oil and garlic in skillet. Add chicken and brown.
2. Remove chicken. Add onions and green pepper; cook until tender. Pour off fat.
3. Return chicken to skillet. Add remaining ingredients. Cover and simmer until chicken is tender.

Serves 6.

Nutrient information per serving:

calories - 175; protein - 20 gm.; carbohydrate - 27 gm.; fat - 3.9 gm.; saturated fat - 0.6 gm.; percentage of calories from fat - 20; sodium - 41.4 mg.; cholesterol - 36 mg.; fiber - 0 gm.

ADA exchange value: 2 lean meat,1 vegetable

Romantic Chicken Dinner

3/4 cup fresh chopped pineapple
1/2 cup sliced green onions
1/8 cup chopped celery
1 Tbsp. grated fresh ginger
2 chicken breasts
1 Tbsp. vegetable oil
3 Tbsp. soy sauce

1. Cover the bottom of a baking dish with pineapple, green onions, celery and ginger. Lay chicken on top.
2. In a small bowl, mix oil and soy sauce. Pour over chicken. Cover and bake for 35 to 40 minutes at 350°.

Makes 2 servings.

Nutrient information per serving:

calories - 277; protein - 35 gm.; carbohydrate - 30 gm.; fat - 11.5 gm.; saturated fat - 2.1 gm.; percentage of calories from fat - 37; sodium - 85 mg.; cholesterol - 85 mg.; fiber - 0 gm.

ADA exchange value: 3 lean meat, 1 fat, 1/2 fruit

Chicken India

4 boned, skinned chicken breast halves
1/3 cup low-fat yogurt
4 tsp. flour
1/8 cup water
1 tsp. curry powder
1/8 tsp. garlic powder
1/8 tsp. paprika
1/8 tsp. lemon pepper
2 10-oz. packages frozen broccoli spears
1/8 cup chopped peanuts

1. Preheat oven to 400°.
2. Place chicken in shallow baking dish. Cover with foil and bake for 20 to 25 minutes.
3. While chicken is baking, combine yogurt and flour; set aside.
4. In a pan, stir together water, curry powder, garlic powder, paprika, and lemon pepper; bring to a boil. Reduce heat and add yogurt mixture. Cook until thickened.
5. Cook broccoli according to package directions; drain. Pour sauce over chicken and top with peanuts; serve with broccoli.

Serves 4.

Nutrient information per serving:

calories - 229; protein - 31 gm.; carbohydrate - 29 gm.; fat - 7 gm.; saturated fat - 1.75 gm.; percentage of calories from fat - 27; sodium - 116 mg.; cholesterol - 76 mg.; fiber - 0 gm.

ADA exchange value: 2 1/2 lean meat,1 vegetable,1 fat

MEDITERRANEAN CHICKEN

1 Tbsp. vegetable oil
4 boneless, skinless chicken breasts, halved
1 Tbsp. margarine
2/3 cup diced onions
3/4 cup low-sodium canned tomatoes
3/4 tsp. basil
1/8 tsp. garlic powder
1/4 tsp. thyme
1/4 cup sweet vermouth

1. In skillet, heat oil and brown chicken on both sides.
2. Transfer chicken to a large saucepan.
3. Melt margarine in same skillet and saute onions; add to chicken in saucepan.
4. Add remaining ingredients to saucepan and simmer for 30 minutes.

Serves 8.

Nutrient information per serving:

calories - 219; protein - 31 gm.; carbohydrate - 15 gm.; fat - 3.75 gm.; saturated fat - 1.4 gm.; percentage of calories from fat - 15; sodium - 28 mg.; cholesterol - 83 mg.; fiber - 0 gm.

ADA exchange value: 3 lean meat

MEAT

Pork With Rosemary

Serve over noodles or rice.

1 lb. pork tenderloin, trimmed, cut into slices
2 medium onions, chopped
1 1/2 cups tomato juice
1 tsp. chopped fresh rosemary (1/2 tsp. dried)
1/8 tsp. cayenne pepper
2 Tbsp. flour, mixed in 1/4 cup water

1. In a heated skillet sprayed with olive oil, slowly drop pieces of pork to brown.
2. Add onions and cook until soft. Add tomato juice and seasonings. Cover and simmer until meat is done (about 20 to 25 minutes).
3. Uncover and add flour mixture. Stir until thick. Serve.

Serves 4.

Nutrient information per serving:

calories - 276; protein - 24 gm.; carbohydrate - 10 gm.; fat - 12 gm.; saturated fat - 4 gm.; percentage of calories from fat - 39; sodium - 354 mg.; cholesterol - 90 mg.; fiber - 1 gm.

ADA exchange value: 4 lean meat, 2 vegetable

Roast Pork With Brown Rice

Pork has really come to be "the other white meat." Pork tenderloin with all fat trimmed off is as low in fat as chicken.

1 lb. tenderloin of pork, all fat trimmed off
1 medium onion, sliced
1 1/2 cups brown rice
3 cups low-salt, fat-free chicken broth
1 1/2 tsp. chicken herb blend (page 44)

1. Spray a Dutch oven with olive oil. Heat on high, and brown all sides of pork. Remove from pan and set aside.
2. Add onion to pan and cook until soft. Add rice and quickly stir for 30 seconds. Turn off heat.
3. Add broth and herb blend to rice and stir. Place pork tenderloin in the pan, cover, and bake in the oven at 350° for 1 hour.
4. Remove pork, slice, and place slices around edges of a serving dish with the rice in the center.

Serves 4.

Nutrient information per serving:

calories - 358; protein - 35 gm.; carbohydrate - 21 gm.; fat - 14 gm.; saturated fat - 5 gm.; percentage of calories from fat - 35; sodium - 451 mg.; cholesterol - 97 mg.; fiber - 1 gm.

ADA exchange value: 4 lean meat, 3/4 starch/bread

Pork Tenderloin With Sage

1/2 cup dry red wine
3 Tbsp. minced green onions
2 Tbsp. minced fresh sage leaves (2 tsp. dried)
1 Tbsp. minced fresh parsley (1 tsp. dried)
1/2 tsp. dried whole thyme
1/2 teaspoon white pepper
2 pork tenderloins (about 3/4 lb. each)
Fresh sage sprigs and parsley for garnish

1. Combine the first six ingredients in a sealable plastic bag. Seal bag and shake well to mix.
2. Trim all fat from pork. Add pork to bag, seal, and shake until pork is well coated with mixture.
3. Marinate pork in the bag in the refrigerator for 8 hours. Turn the bag occasionally.
4. Remove the pork from the marinade and place the marinade in a small saucepan. Bring marinade to a boil and cook 5 minutes.
5. Place pork on a rack in a roasting pan coated with cooking spray. Bake at 400° for 45 minutes or until meat is well done. (Use a meat thermometer if you have one and when the thermometer shows the center of the meat has been heated to 170°, it's done.) Baste the pork frequently with the heated marinade.
6. Transfer the tenderloins to a serving platter. Let meat stand for 10 minutes, then slice diagonally across the grain into thin slices.
7. Garnish with fresh sage and parsley sprigs and serve.

Serves 6.

Nutrient information per serving:

calories - 141; protein - 23.9 gm.; carbohydrate - 0.7 gm.; fat - 4.1 gm.; saturated fat - 1 gm.; percentage of calories from fat - 26; sodium - 58 mg.; cholesterol - 77 mg.; fiber - 1 gm.

ADA exchange value: 4 lean meat

Rack Of Lamb With Mustard

When you serve this succulent dish, be sure to divide the mustard crust so there is some with each portion. It adds a wonderful flavor!

2 lb. rack of lamb (Ask your butcher to trim off all the fat.)
1/2 cup dry bread crumbs
1 clove garlic, minced
1/2 tsp. dry thyme
1/4 tsp. freshly ground black pepper
4 Tbsp. Dijon mustard

1. Preheat the oven to 400°.
2. Combine all ingredients, except lamb, and rub over the lamb.
3. Roast lamb for 45 to 60 minutes, to desired doneness.

Serves 6.

Nutrient information per serving:

calories - 241; protein - 31 gm.; carbohydrate - 7 gm.; fat - 9 gm.; saturated fat - 5 gm.; percentage of calories from fat - 33; sodium - 265 mg.; cholesterol - 106 mg.; fiber - 0 gm.

ADA exchange value: 4 medium fat meat

Lamb Chops 'N' Herb Sauce

6 lean lamb loin chops (about 6 oz. each, about 1-in.thick)
1/2 cup dry vermouth
1/4 cup chopped fresh parsley
1 Tbsp. chopped fresh basil
2 tsp. grated lemon rind
1 tsp. grated orange rind
1/4 tsp. ground white pepper
1/8 tsp. garlic powder
Lemon or orange wedges
Fresh basil sprigs to garnish

1. Trim all fat from chops. Place chops in large shallow dish.
2. Combine vermouth and next six ingredients; stir well. Pour vermouth mixture over chops then cover and marinate in refrigerator 8 hours, turning occasionally.
3. Remove chops from marinade and reserve marinade.
4. Coat a large nonstick skillet with cooking spray. Place over medium-high heat until hot. Add chops and cook 4 minutes on each side or until browned.
5. Remove chops from skillet; drain and pat dry with paper towels. Wipe drippings from skillet with a paper towel. Return chops to skillet and pour reserved marinade over chops.
6. Bring mixture to a boil over medium heat; cover, reduce heat, and simmer 20 minutes or until chops are tender. Transfer chops to a serving platter, using a slotted spoon.
7. Garnish with lemon or orange wedges and fresh basil sprigs, and serve.

Serves 6.

Nutrient information per serving:

calories - 190; protein - 25.6 gm.; carbohydrate - 1.3 gm.; fat - 8.4 gm.; saturated fat - 5 gm.; percentage of calories from fat - 40; sodium - 75 mg.; cholesterol - 81 mg.; fiber - 0 gm.

ADA exchange value: 4 medium-fat meat

Old Fashioned Beef Stew

Serve this with a green salad and some crusty French bread and you'll have a great meal. This recipe can also be cooked in your crock pot for 8 hours on low.

1 lb. very lean beef, cut in large cubes
2 10-oz. pkg. frozen stew vegetables
1 can of low-fat, low-salt tomato soup
1 1/2 tsp. basic herb blend (page 44)

1. Preheat oven to 300°.
2. In a casserole dish, mix all ingredients, cover, and bake for 3 hours.

Serves 6.

Nutrient information per serving:

calories - 259; protein - 22 gm.; carbohydrate -30 gm.; fat - 5 gm.; saturated fat - 2 gm.; percentage of calories from fat - 17; sodium - 451 mg.; cholesterol - 48 mg.; fiber - 0 gm.

ADA exchange value: 3 lean meat, 2 vegetable, 1/2 starch/bread

GERMAN VEAL SCHNITZEL

1 lb. veal cutlets
2 Tbsp. all-purpose flour
1 tsp. minced fresh parsley
1/2 tsp. white pepper
1/4 tsp. paprika
1/8 tsp. ground cloves
cooking spray
1 tsp. canola oil, divided
1 1/2 tsp. fresh parsley, minced
Lemon slices to garnish

1. Trim all fat from cutlets and place them between 2 sheets of heavy-duty plastic wrap. Use a meat mallet to flatten cutlets to 1/8-inch thickness.
2. Combine flour and next four ingredients; stir well. Dredge cutlets in flour mixture.
3. Coat a large nonstick skillet with cooking spray. Add 1/2 tsp. oil. Place over medium-high heat until hot.
4. Add half of cutlets to skillet; cook 2 to 4 minutes on each side, until lightly browned. Wipe drippings from skillet with paper towel. Then repeat procedure using other 1/2 tsp. oil and remaining cutlets.
5. Transfer cutlets to individual serving plates and sprinkle with parsley. Garnish with lemon slices.

Serves 4.

Nutrient information per serving:

calories - 154; protein - 23.3 gm.; carbohydrate - 3.1 gm.; fat - 5 gm.; saturated fat - 2 gm.; percentage of calories from fat - 29; sodium - 98 mg.; cholesterol - 94 mg.; fiber - 0 gm.

ADA exchange value: 4 medium-fat meat

Chateaubriand

This can either be roasted or barbecued.

1 lb. beef tenderloin, all fat trimmed off
1 tsp. tarragon
1/2 tsp. freshly ground black pepper

1. Sprinkle beef with tarragon and pepper and pound.
2. Roast in oven preheated to 400° for 20 minutes or to desired doneness.

Serves 4.

Nutrient information per serving:

calories - 240; protein - 34 gm.; carbohydrate - 0 gm.; fat - 10 gm.; saturated fat - 4 gm.; percentage of calories from fat - 39; sodium - 76 mg.; cholesterol - 100 mg.; fiber - 0 gm.

ADA exchange value: 4 medium-fat meat

MEATLOAF

If you don't have a special meatloaf pan—one with holes that fits into another pan so the fat can drip out—take a foil loaf pan and poke holes in it. Make a few balls of foil and put them in the bottom of a regular loaf pan. Place the foil pan inside the regular pan for baking.

1 lb. very lean ground beef
1 lb. ground turkey
3 egg whites
1 cup rolled oats
1/2 cup ketchup
2 tsp. dry mustard
1/2 tsp. ground black pepper
1/2 tsp. basic herb blend (page 43)
1/2 tsp. paprika
1 medium onion, diced
1 green bell pepper, diced
1 red bell pepper, diced

TOPPING

1/4 cup ketchup
1/4 cup Dijon mustard

1. Preheat oven to 350°.
2. Combine all ingredients except topping.
3. Put in a loaf pan that has been sprayed with a nonstick spray.
4. Mix ketchup and mustard together and spread over the top.
5. Bake for 2 hours.

Serves 6.

Nutrient information per serving:

calories - 338; protein - 45 gm.; carbohydrate - 17 gm.; fat - 9 gm.; saturated fat - 3 gm.; percentage of calories from fat - 24; sodium - 449 mg.; cholesterol - 101 mg.; fiber - 3 gm.

ADA exchange value: 5 lean meat, 1 starch/bread

Ground Beef With Rice

This is a great way to use up leftovers. You could replace the beef with chicken or turkey and use just about any left-over vegetable.

1/2 lb. lean ground beef
1/2 medium onion, chopped
1/2 green bell pepper, chopped
1/2 red bell pepper, chopped
1 1/2 tsp. Italian herb blend (page 43)
1 28 oz. can diced tomatoes
3 cups cooked brown rice

1. In a large nonstick skillet, saute beef until well cooked. Set aside on paper plate to drain.
2. Spray skillet with nonstick spray, and cook onion and peppers until soft. Add seasonings and tomatoes and simmer 10 minutes, uncovered.
3. Return beef to skillet and add rice. Mix well and heat through.

Serves 4.

Nutrient information per serving:

calories - 315; protein - 15 gm.; carbohydrate - 47 gm.; fat - 7 gm.; saturated fat - 3 gm.; percentage of calories from fat - 21; sodium - 369 mg.; cholesterol - 32 mg.; fiber - 4 gm.

ADA exchange value: 2 starch/bread, 2 vegetable, 1 medium fat meat, 1/2 fat

Flank Steak Grilled With An Indian Flair

This is good served with steamed white or brown rice, with chutney on the side.

1 1/2 lb. flank steak, trimmed of all fat
1/2 tsp. freshly ground black pepper
1 tsp. cayenne pepper
1/2 tsp. allspice
1/2 tsp. cumin
1/2 tsp. turmeric

1. Rinse the flank steak and pat dry.
2. Mix all the herbs and spices together and spread them over the steak. Using a mallet, pound the herbs into the meat.
3. Spray the meat lightly with olive oil. Either barbecue or broil meat for 1 to 2 minutes on each side.
4. Cut on the diagonal and serve.

Serves 6.

Nutrient information per serving:

calories - 165; protein - 27 gm.; carbohydrate - 0 gm.; fat - 5 gm.; saturated fat - 2 gm.; percentage of calories from fat - 27; sodium - 151 mg.; cholesterol - 72 mg.; fiber - 0 gm.

ADA exchange value: 4 lean meat

Beef Kabobs

1 1/2 lbs. lean beef, cut into 1-inch cubes
2 tsp. minced garlic
1/4 cup minced onion
1/3 cup lemon juice
1/2 tsp. dry mustard
3/4 tsp. chili powder
1/8 tsp. pepper
2 tsp. honey
3/4 tsp. ginger
1 tsp. allspice

1. Place meat in mixing bowl.
2. Combine remaining ingredients and pour over meat; mix thoroughly. Let stand for 1 hour.
3. Thread meat on skewers. Broil, turning occasionally, until desired doneness is achieved.

Serves 4.

Nutrient information per serving:

calories - 254; protein - 28 gm.; carbohydrate - 0 gm.; fat - 13 gm.; saturated fat - 4.25 gm.; percentage of calories from fat - 46; sodium - 102 mg.; cholesterol - 185 mg.; fiber - 0 gm.

ADA exchange value: 3 meat

Dilled Round Steak

1 lb. beef round steak
3/4 cup water
2/3 cup sliced onions
2 tsp. lime juice
1/2 tsp. instant beef bouillon granules
1/2 tsp. garlic powder
1 tsp. fresh dillweed or 1/2 tsp. dried dillweed
1/8 tsp. freshly ground black pepper
1 Tbsp. cornstarch mixed with 2 Tbsp. water

1. Cut meat into 4 servings. In nonstick skillet, brown meat on medium-high heat.
2. Add water, onion, lime juice, bouillon granules, garlic powder, dillweed, and pepper to skillet. Bring to a boil, then reduce heat. Cover and simmer for 30 to 40 minutes.
3. Stir cornstarch mixture into juices. Cook until thick and bubbly.

Serves 4.

Nutrient information per serving:

calories - 185; protein - 32 gm.; carbohydrate - 3 gm.; fat - 5.3 gm.; saturated fat - 1.9 gm.; percentage of calories from fat - 25; sodium - 271 mg.; cholesterol - 72mg.; fiber - 0 gm.

ADA exchange value: 4 meat

Green Pepper Steak

1/2 lb. lean roundsteak
1/8 cup soy sauce
1 tsp. minced garlic
1/8 tsp. ground ginger
2 Tbsp. vegetable oil
1/2 cup chopped green onions
1/2 cup chopped red pepper
1/2 cup chopped celery
1 tsp. cornstarch
1/2 cup water
2 cups cooked rice

1. Cut beef into thin strips. Combine soy sauce, garlic, and ginger; mix. Add beef and toss.
2. Heat oil in skillet. Add beef mixture and stir-fry over high heat until brown. Cover and simmer until meat is tender.
3. Turn up heat and add vegetables, stir-frying until crisp-tender.
4. Mix cornstarch with water; add to skillet. Stir and cook until thickened. Serve with rice.

Serves 4.

Nutrient information per serving:

calories - 260; protein - 30 gm.; carbohydrate - 3 gm.; fat - 12.1 gm.; saturated fat - 2.75 gm.; percentage of calories from fat - 42; sodium - 675 mg.; cholesterol - 38.5 mg.; fiber - 0 gm.

ADA exchange value: 2 meat, 1 vegetable, 1 starch/bread

Roast Beef With Herb Sauce

This one has a few more steps and takes a little more time, but for special occasions, believe me, it's worth that extra effort.

1 beef eye-of-round roast (about 3 lbs.)
1/2 tsp. dried whole marjoram
1/4 tsp. dried whole thyme
1/4 tsp. white pepper
1/8 tsp. garlic powder
2 cups water
1 tsp. canola oil
1/2 cup onion, chopped fine
1/2 cup celery, chopped fine
2 cloves garlic, minced
1 jar sliced pimento, undrained (4 ounces)
1/4 cup red wine vinegar
1/4 cup chopped fresh chives
3 Tbsp. chopped fresh parsley (1 1/2 tsp. dried)
1 Tbsp. chopped fresh sage (1/2 Tbsp. dried)
1/4 tsp. salt
1/4 tsp. black pepper
Fresh parsley sprigs to garnish
Fresh sage sprigs to garnish

1. Trim all fat from the roast.
2. Combine marjoram, thyme, 1/4 teaspoon white pepper, and garlic powder. Rub the mixture over entire surface of the meat.
3. Place roast on a rack of a broiler pan coated with cooking spray. Pour water into broiler pan, cover roast with aluminum foil, and bake at 450° for 20 minutes.
4. Uncover and bake for 1 to 1 1/2 hours more. (If you use a meat thermometer, the reading should be 140° for rare or 160° for medium.)

5. Let the roast stand for 15 minutes then slice it diagonally across the grain into thin slices. Transfer the roast to a large serving platter and keep it warm.
6. In a small saucepan, heat canola oil over medium-high heat until hot. Add chopped onion, chopped celery, and minced garlic. Saute until tender.
7. Add pimento, vinegar, chopped chives, chopped parsley, and sage. Stir well to combine. Add salt and pepper, and stir well again. Cook 2 to 3 minutes until heated through.
8. Spoon herb sauce evenly over each serving of roast. Garnish roast with fresh parsley and sage sprigs.

Serves 12.

Nutrient information per serving:

calories - 162; protein - 24 gm.; carbohydrate -1.6 gm.; fat - 6 gm.; saturated fat - 2 gm.; percentage of calories from fat - 33; sodium - 108 mg.; cholesterol - 56 mg.; fiber - 1 gm.

ADA exchange value: 2 medium-fat meat

BEANS

A NOTE ABOUT BEANS

Beans are an excellent source of protein and fiber. As a bonus, they have no fat at all! It is always better to cook dried beans, if you have a choice. You can cook a large pot of beans and then freeze portions of 1 or 2 cups in individual containers for use in other recipes later. You'll always have them available when you need them this way. As a second choice, keep a can of beans in your pantry and before you use them, rinse them in a colander under cold water to remove the excess sodium.

The best way to cook dried beans is to soak them overnight. Rinse them the next day and put them in a large pot of water. Bring to a boil, rinse again in a colander under cold water, then put the beans back in the pot. Cover beans with water or broth. Add a couple of bay leaves and simmer until the beans are tender, approximately 1 to 2 hours. Remove bay leaves. You have great beans without too much of the starch. It is the starch that can cause stomach gas.

Navy Bean And Basil Salad

1/2 cup low-sodium chicken broth
1/4 cup red wine vinegar
3 shallots, chopped
1/4 cup freshly chopped basil
3 cups cooked navy beans
2 oz. sliced black olives
3 ripe tomatoes, chopped
6 large red lettuce leaves

1. In a saucepan, combine broth, vinegar, and shallots and bring to a boil. Reduce to simmer.
2. Add basil, beans, olives and stir well. Cover and turn off heat. Let stand 10 minutes. (You may also remove and chill in refrigerator if you prefer a cold salad.)
3. Place lettuce leaves on salad plates, spoon bean mixture onto leaves, then top with chopped tomato.

Serves 6.

Nutrient information per serving:

calories - 136; protein - 8 gm.; carbohydrate - 24 gm.; fat - 1 gm.; saturated fat - 0 gm.; percentage of calories from fat - 1; sodium - 493 mg.; cholesterol - 0 mg.; fiber - 5 gm.

ADA exchange value: 2 starch/bread, 1 vegetable

Black-And-White Bean Salad

3 cups cooked black beans
3 cups cooked navy beans
1 yellow bell pepper, chopped
2 oz. can Ortega® chilies, chopped
1/2 red onion, chopped fine
1/2 cup fresh cilantro, chopped
1/2 tsp. freshly ground black pepper
1/8 tsp. crushed red pepper (or to taste)
1/4 cup white-wine vinegar
1 head iceberg lettuce, chopped fine

Mix all ingredients and toss well. Serve.

Serves 8.

Nutrient information per serving:

calories - 175; protein - 11 gm.; carbohydrate - 32 gm.; fat - 1 gm.; saturated fat - 0 gm.; percentage of calories from fat - 0; sodium - 714 mg.; cholesterol - 0 mg.; fiber - 6 gm.

ADA exchange value: 2 starch/vegetable

Pepper-Bean Burritos

1/2 cup chopped onion
1 clove garlic, minced
1 cup chopped sweet red peppers
1 cup chopped sweet yellow peppers
1 jalapeno pepper, seeded and diced
1 15-oz. can kidney beans, rinsed and drained
1/2 tsp. ground cumin
6 flour tortillas (6-inch size)
1 cup chopped tomato
3/4 cup shredded reduced-fat Monterey Jack cheese
6 cups shredded iceberg lettuce
1/4 cup plus 2 Tbsp. low-fat sour cream

1. Coat large nonstick skillet with nonstick spray. Place over medium-high heat until hot. Then add onion, garlic, and peppers; saute until tender, and set aside.
2. Mash kidney beans with potato masher and stir in cumin. Spread kidney bean mixture evenly over tortillas.
3. Mix sweet and jalapeno peppers. Top tortillas evenly with pepper mixture.
4. Sprinkle chopped tomatoes over peppers.
5. Top each tortilla with 2 Tbsp. cheese. Roll tortillas up and secure with toothpicks. Place seam side up in a baking dish coated with nonstick spray. Cover and bake for 20 minutes at 350°.

To serve, remove toothpicks. Place 1 cup shredded lettuce on each serving plate and place burritos on lettuce. Serve each burrito with 1 Tbsp. low-fat sour cream.

Serves 6.

Nutrient information per serving:

calories - 232; protein - 11 gm.; carbohydrate - 34 gm.; fat - 7 gm.; saturated fat - 0 gm.; percentage of calories from fat - 28; sodium - 94 mg.; cholesterol - 16 mg.; fiber -3 gm.

ADA exchange value: 2 starch/bread, 1 vegetable

Navy Bean Soup

Old-fashioned navy bean soup like this can be served with a big salad and a side of chili cornbread.

1 medium onion, chopped
1/4 lb. Canadian bacon, chopped
2 carrots, chopped
2 celery stalks, chopped
1 tsp. marjoram
1 tsp. chervil
1/4 tsp. crushed red pepper
3 cups low-sodium chicken broth
1 14-oz. can diced tomatoes in juice
5 cups cooked navy beans

1. In a large Dutch oven sprayed with olive oil, saute onions until soft. Add Canadian bacon, carrots, celery, and saute, stirring constantly for 2 minutes.
2. Add remaining ingredients and simmer for 30 minutes.
3. Put 1 cup of the soup in a food processor or blender and blend until smooth. Add back to soup to thicken.

Serves 8.

Nutrient information per serving:

calories - 207; protein - 16 gm.; carbohydrate - 34 gm.; fat - 2 gm.; saturated fat - 1 gm.; percentage of calories from fat - 7; sodium - 361 mg.; cholesterol - 6 mg.; fiber - 6 gm.

ADA exchange value: 2 starch/bread, 1 lean meat

Bahamian Beans And Rice

1 1/2 tsp. olive oil
1 roasted red bell pepper, julienned
1/2 green bell pepper, julienned
2 cloves garlic, finely chopped
2 16-oz. cans black beans, drained and rinsed
2 Tbsp. distilled white vinegar
8 dashes Tabasco sauce
3 cups cooked white rice
3 Tbsp. fresh cilantro, chopped fine
Salt and freshly ground pepper to taste

1. In large saute pan, heat oil over medium-high heat until hot, but not smoking.
2. Add red and green pepper, and garlic. Saute two minutes.
3. Add black beans, vinegar, and Tabasco. Bring the mixture to a boil, then reduce heat to low, cover, and simmer for 5 minutes.
4. Stir in rice and cilantro, and serve.

Serves 6.

Nutrient information per serving:

calories - 229; protein - 9 gm.; carbohydrate - 44 gm.; fat - 2 gm.; saturated fat - 0 gm.; percentage of calories from fat - 1; sodium - 3 mg.; cholesterol - 0 mg.; fiber -3 gm.

ADA exchange value: 2 starch/bread, 1 vegetable

Lentil Stew

Lentils are quick to cook and a good source of protein and fiber. With a big salad on the side and a loaf of crusty bread, you have a nutritious and tasty meal.

1 cup dry lentils
3 1/2 cups low-sodium chicken broth
1 14 1/2-oz. can diced tomatoes
1 potato, washed and cubed
2 carrots, chopped
2 celery stalks, chopped
1 Tbsp. basil
1/2 tsp. chervil
1/2 tsp. onion powder
1/2 tsp. garlic powder
1/8 tsp. crushed red pepper

1. Rinse and drain lentils.
2. In a large saucepan, combine all ingredients. Bring to a boil. Reduce heat and simmer, covered, for 45 minutes or until done.

Serves 4.

Nutrient information per serving:

calories - 187; protein - 13 gm.; carbohydrate - 34 gm.; fat - 1gm.; saturated fat - 1 gm;. percentage of calories from fat - 3; sodium - 327 mg.; cholesterol - 0 mg.; fiber - 7 gm.

ADA exchange value: 2 starch/bread, 1 vegetable

RED BEANS AND RICE SALAD

This makes a good luncheon dish, or serve it as the main entree for supper. Serve on lettuce leaves with Cheese Monkey Bread (recipe on page 225).

8 sun-dried tomatoes
1/2 cup low-sodium chicken broth
3 cups cooked red beans
3 cups cooked brown rice
1/2 cucumber, chopped
1 red bell pepper, chopped
3 celery stalks, chopped
3 scallions, chopped
1/4 cup red-wine vinegar
2 Tbsp. prepared mustard
1/2 tsp. thyme
1/2 tsp. marjoram
1/2 tsp. chervil
1/8 tsp. cayenne pepper

1. In a saucepan, bring chicken broth to a boil. Add tomatoes, cover, turn heat off, and let stand for 10 minutes. Remove tomatoes and rinse under cold water. Chop tomatoes.
2. Mix broth, tomatoes, and all other ingredients in a serving dish. Cover and refrigerate at least 30 minutes before serving.

Serves 6.

Nutrient information per serving:

calories - 195; protein - 9 gm.; carbohydrate - 37 gm.; fat - 1 gm.; saturated fat - 0 gm.; percentage of calories from fat - 1; sodium - 614 mg.; cholesterol - 0 mg.; fiber - 5 gm.

ADA exchange value: 2 starch/bread, 1 vegetable

Black Bean Spread

This spread can be used on many things: crackers, celery, bread. My favorite, however, is to take a large flour tortilla (check the label when you buy tortillas and buy the one with the least fat), spread the bean spread on the tortilla, roll it up, refrigerate for 2 hours, then slice. These make an attractive appetizer and are really fun to have on hand for company.

4 cups cooked black beans
1/2 cup salsa
1/8 tsp. cayenne pepper
1/4 cup fresh cilantro

1. Put all ingredients, except cilantro, in food processor with steel blade. Process until smooth.
2. Add cilantro and pulse processor until cilantro is just mixed in.
3. Place in a covered container and refrigerate.

Serves 8.

Nutrient information per serving:

calories - 30; protein - 2 gm.; carbohydrate - 6 gm.; fat - 0 gm.; saturated fat - 0 gm.; percentage of calories from fat - 6; sodium - 134 mg.; cholesterol - 0 mg.; fiber - 1 gm.

ADA exchange value: 1/2 starch/bread

VEGETABLES

Eggplant Entree

For times when you want to pretend you're having a steak, but you really need to stick with vegetables, here's an interesting variation on an eggplant theme. Be careful, though, this one is higher in fat, even though it's low in calories.

2 eggplants (1 1/2 lbs. total), ends trimmed,
  cut crosswise into 3/4- in.-thick slices
2 tsp. salt
1 Tbsp. olive oil, extra virgin
2 Tbsp. balsamic vinegar
1 Tbsp. chopped fresh mint
1/2 tsp. dried oregano
1 small clove garlic, minced
Freshly ground black pepper to taste

1. Sprinkle eggplant with salt and drain in colander for 30 minutes.
2. Preheat oven to 450°. Lightly coat two baking sheets with nonstick cooking spray.
3. Rinse eggplant under cold water and pat dry. Arrange the slices in a single layer on the baking sheets.
4. Bake for 20 minutes, then turn eggplant over and bake 5 minutes longer, or until eggplant is golden brown and tender.
5. In a small bowl, stir together oil, vinegar, mint, oregano, and garlic.
6. Season the eggplant with pepper and brush tops with the oil mixture.

Serve at room temperature.

Serves 6.

Nutrient information per serving:

calories - 40; protein - 1 gm.; carbohydrate - 2 gm.; fat - 2 gm.; saturated fat - 0 gm.; percentage of calories from fat - 65; sodium - 2 mg.; cholesterol - 0 mg.; fiber - 0 gm.

ADA exchange value: 1 starch/bread

Mushrooms Paprika

This can be served over rice as a side dish or over broiled chicken or pork.

1 Tbsp. shallots, chopped fine
1 lb. mushrooms, sliced
1 tsp. fresh lemon juice
2 tsp. paprika
1/8 tsp. ground red pepper
1/2 cup low-fat sour cream

1. In a skillet sprayed with nonstick spray, saute shallots until soft. Add mushrooms and lemon juice; cover and simmer for 3 minutes.
2. Remove cover and saute until all liquid is absorbed.
3. Mix paprika and red pepper into sour cream. Add to mushrooms and heat (do not boil).

Serves 4.

Nutrient information per serving:

calories - 66; protein - 3 gm.; carbohydrate - 8 gm.; fat - 2 gm.; saturated fat - 0 gm.; percentage of calories from fat - 33; sodium - 25 mg.; cholesterol - 10 mg.; fiber - 3 gm.

ADA exchange value: 2 vegetable

Vegetarian Main Dish

Here's one for meatless days. It is delicious, but it does take a little extra time to prepare.

1/2 package commercial coleslaw vegetable mix (about 8 ounces total)
1 cup fresh mushrooms, sliced
1/2 cup yellow squash, quartered and thinly sliced
1/2 cup zucchini, quartered and thinly sliced
3/4 cup canned, cooked black beans, drained and rinsed
1/2 tsp. dried basil
1/4 tsp. dried thyme
1/4 tsp. onion powder
1/4 tsp. garlic powder
1/8 tsp. salt
1/8 tsp. black pepper
1 Tbsp. reduced-calorie margarine
1/2 cup all-purpose flour
1/2 cup skim milk
2 eggs, beaten
1/2 cup shredded provolone cheese

1. Spray a large nonstick skillet with cooking spray. Place over medium-high heat until hot.

2. Add slaw mix, mushrooms, squash, and zucchini, and saute 5 to 7 minutes until vegetables are tender. Stir frequently.

3. Add black beans and next 6 ingredients. Remove from heat and keep warm.

4. Coat a 9-inch pie plate with nonstick spray and add margarine. Bake at 425° for 1 minute until margarine melts.

5. Combine flour, milk, and eggs in a medium bowl; stir well with a wire whisk. Pour mixture into prepared pie plate. Do not stir.

6. Bake at 425° for 15 to 20 minutes or until puffed and browned.

7. Spoon vegetable mixture into shell. Sprinkle with cheese, and bake 1 to 2 minutes until cheese melts. Serve immediately.

Serves 4.

Nutrient information per serving:

calories - 240; protein - 14 gm.; carbohydrate - 28 gm.; fat - 9 gm.; saturated fat - 3 gm.; percentage of calories from fat - 34; sodium - 287 mg.; cholesterol - 110 mg.; fiber - 4 gm.

ADA exchange value: 1 vegetable, 1/2 fat

Green Beans Vinaigrette

1 Tbsp. Dijon mustard
3 Tbsp. herb vinegar
2 tsp. olive oil
1/4 cup water
1 tsp. fresh lemon juice
1/2 tsp. vegetable herb blend (page 44)
1/2 tsp. sugar
Freshly ground pepper to taste
1 1/2 lb. fresh green beans, trimmed
6 large lettuce cups for garnish

1. Combine everything except beans and lettuce and set aside.
2. Steam beans until just tender. Place in a bowl and pour vinaigrette over them. Mix well, cover, and refrigerate for at least 2 hours.
3. Serve in large lettuce cups.

Serves 6.

Nutrient information per serving:

calories - 46; protein - 2 gm.; carbohydrate - 7 gm.; fat - 2 gm.; saturated fat - 0 gm.; percentage of calories from fat - 35; sodium - 48 mg.; cholesterol - 0 mg.; fiber - 3 gm.

ADA exchange value: 1 vegetable, 1/2 fat

Herbed Green Beans

Here's a really quick way to make a healthy, herby side dish in the microwave. It's ready in a flash.

1/2 lb. fresh green beans
1/2 cup water
1/4 cup chopped sweet green pepper
1/4 cup sliced green onions
3/4 cup peeled, diced tomato
1 tsp. fresh basil, minced (1/2 tsp. dried)
1 tsp. lemon juice
1/4 tsp. salt
1/4 tsp. sugar
1/4 tsp. fresh rosemary, minced

1. Wash beans and remove strings. Cut beans into 1 1/2-inch pieces.
2. Combine beans and water in a 1 1/2-quart casserole. Cover with heavy-duty plastic wrap and microwave on high for 4 to 5 minutes or until green beans are crisp-tender, stirring after 4 minutes. Let stand, covered, 2 minutes, then drain well.
3. Combine chopped green peppers and sliced green onions in a 1-cup glass measure. Stir well to mix. Cover with heavy-duty plastic wrap and microwave on high for to 2 minutes or until tender.
4. Add green pepper mixture, tomato, basil, lemon juice, salt, sugar, and rosemary to green beans. Stir gently to combine. Cover with plastic wrap and microwave on high for 1 minute or until heated through.

Serves 4.

Nutrient information per serving:

calories - 27; protein - 1 gm.; carbohydrate - 6 gm.; fat - 0.2 gm.; saturated fat - 0 gm.; percentage of calories from fat - 1; sodium - 151 mg.; cholesterol - 0 mg.; fiber - 3 gm.

ADA exchange value: 1 vegetable

Potatoes And Carrots

12 whole tiny new potatoes, washed
4 medium carrots, washed and cut in 1-inch slices on the diagonal
2 tsp. Butter Buds® mixed in 2 Tbsp. hot water
1 tsp. vegetable herb blend

1. Steam potatoes and carrots, covered, for 20 minutes.
2. Put in serving dish and toss with Butter Buds and herbs.

Serves 4.

Nutrient information per serving:

calories - 127; protein - 3 gm.; carbohydrate - 28 gm.; fat - 0 gm.; saturated fat - 0 gm.; percentage of calories from fat - 0; sodium - 67 mg.; cholesterol - 0 mg.; fiber - 3 gm.

ADA exchange value: 1 vegetable, 1 starch/bread

Artichokes

These are great served warm or cold.

4 medium artichokes, cut off stems and tops with kitchen shears, trim the leaves
1 cup water
1/2 tsp. vegetable herb blend (page 44)

1. Bring water to a boil and add vegetable herb blend.
2. Place artichokes in water, reduce heat to simmer, and cover, leaving a steam vent.
3. Cook 45 minutes.

Serves 4.

Nutrient information per serving:

calories - 53; protein - 3 gm.; carbohydrate - 12 gm.; fat - 0 gm.; saturated fat - 0 gm.; percentage of calories from fat - 0; sodium - 79 mg.; cholesterol - 0 mg.; fiber - 4 gm.

ADA exchange value: 1 vegetable

Brussels Sprouts

These are both tasty and low in calories. You can hold the cooked Brussels sprouts and heat them in the herbed butter sauce just before serving. They are also good cold.

20 medium Brussels sprouts
1 tsp. low-calorie margarine
1/2 tsp. vegetable herb blend (page 44)

1. Steam or microwave Brussels sprouts until they are tender.
2. In a medium-sized saucepan, melt margarine. Add herb blend.
3. Place Brussels sprouts in saucepan and stir until all are covered.

Serves 4.

Nutrient information per serving:

calories - 49; protein - 3 gm.; carbohydrate - 8 gm.; fat - 1 gm.; saturated fat - 0 gm.; percentage of calories from fat - 18; sodium - 33 mg.; cholesterol - 0 mg.; fiber - 2 gm.

ADA exchange value: 2 vegetable

Fried Green Tomatoes

1/4 cup corn meal
1/4 tsp. salt
1/4 tsp. freshly ground pepper
1/2 tsp. vegetable blend (page 44)
1 tsp. sugar
2 egg whites beaten
2 Tbsp. water
4 green tomatoes, sliced 1/2-inch thick

1. Preheat oven to 450°.
2. Combine cornmeal, salt, pepper, vegetable blend, and sugar.
3. Whip together egg whites and water.
4. Dip tomatoes in egg mixture then into cornmeal mixture.
5. Place tomatoes on cookie sheet sprayed with olive oil. Lightly spray top of tomatoes.
6. Bake for 10 to 12 minutes until lightly browned.

Serves 6.

Nutrient information per serving:

calories - 44; protein - 2 gm.; carbohydrate - 4 gm.; fat - 0 gm.; saturated fat - 0 gm.; percentage of calories from fat -0; sodium - 115 mg.; cholesterol - 0 mg.; fiber - 1 gm.

ADA exchange value: 1 1/2 vegetable

Stir-Fried Zucchini And Yellow Squash

1 tsp. olive oil
1/2 onion, sliced thin
2 medium zucchini, sliced
2 medium yellow squash, sliced
1 Tbsp. chopped fresh basil (or 1 tsp. dried)
1/8 tsp. crushed red pepper
Freshly ground pepper to taste

1. In a nonstick skillet sprayed with nonstick spray, heat olive oil. Add onions and cook until soft. Add garlic and stir in for 30 seconds.
2. Add zucchini and yellow squash and stir fry until tender. Add basil and pepper.

Serves 4.

Nutrient information per serving:

calories - 54; protein - 1 gm.; carbohydrate - 10 gm.; fat - 2 gm.; saturated fat - 0 gm.; percentage of calories from fat - 19; sodium - 1 mg.; cholesterol - 0 mg.; fiber - 3 gm.

ADA exchange value: 2 vegetable

Tri-Colored Peppers

This dish can be used to add color and flavor to a variety of dishes.

1 green bell pepper, sliced
1 red bell pepper, sliced
1 yellow bell pepper, sliced
1 onion, sliced
1 tsp. vegetable herb blend (page 44)

1. Spray a large skillet with olive oil. Add all ingredients to pan and stir over high heat for 30 seconds.
2. Add 1/4 cup water to pan. Cover and reduce heat to low. Simmer for 10 minutes. Remove cover. Bring heat to medium high and cook until all liquid is absorbed.

Serves 6.

Nutrient information per serving:

calories - 15; protein - 0 gm.; carbohydrate - 3 gm.; fat - 0 gm.; saturated fat - 0 gm.; percentage of calories from fat - 12; sodium - 1 mg.; cholesterol - 0 mg.; fiber - 1 gm.

ADA exchange value: 1 vegetable

Carrots With Artichoke Hearts And Mushrooms

1 lb. mushrooms, washed and cut in quarters
2 Tbsp. dry vermouth
1 shallot, minced
9-oz. pkg. frozen artichoke hearts, cooked
3 cups baby carrots, cooked
1/3 cup low-salt chicken stock
2 tsp. vegetable herb blend (page 44)

1 Tbsp. fresh parsley, chopped

1. In nonstick skillet sprayed with nonstick spray, place mushrooms with vermouth. Cover and simmer 3 minutes. Uncover, add shallots, and saute until all liquid is absorbed.
2. Add remaining ingredients, except parsley. Cook slowly until all liquid is absorbed. Toss with parsley and serve.

Serves 6.

Nutrient information per serving:

calories - 68; protein - 3 gm.; carbohydrate - 14 gm.; fat - 0 gm.; saturated fat - 0 gm.; percentage of calories from fat - 0; sodium - 122 mg.; cholesterol - 0 mg.; fiber - 5 gm.

ADA exchange value: 3 vegetable

Lemon Herbed Asparagus

1 lb. asparagus spears, rinsed and trimmed
2 tsp. Butter Buds® mixed in 2 Tbsp. hot water
1/4 tsp. dried basil
1/4 tsp. oregano
2 tsp. fresh lemon juice

1. Steam asparagus in steamer for 5 minutes.
2. In saucepan, mix Butter Buds, herbs, and lemon juice. Heat on low, add asparagus, and toss gently to cover. Serve warm or cold.

Serves 4.

Nutrient information per serving:

calories - 35; protein - 3 gm.; carbohydrate - 6 gm.; fat - 0 gm.; saturated fat - 0 gm.; percentage of calories from fat - 0; sodium - 41 mg.; cholesterol - 0 mg. fiber - 2 gm.

ADA exchange value: 1 vegetable

Dilled Carrots

These are good served cold as a snack or as a garnish for a salad.

1 lb. baby carrots
1/2 cup white-wine vinegar
1/2 cup water
1 tsp. dill weed
1/2 tsp. celery seed
1/2 tsp. basil

1. Wash carrots.
2. Place all ingredients in a saucepan. Bring to a boil, reduce heat, cover, and simmer for 15 minutes.
3. Chill for several hours or overnight in liquid.
4. Drain and keep carrots in refrigerator in a covered container until you are ready to serve them.

Serves 6.

Nutrient information per serving:

calories - 35; protein - 1 gm.; carbohydrate - 9 gm.; fat - 0 gm.; saturated fat - 0 gm.; percentage of calories from fat - 3; sodium - 26 mg.; cholesterol - 0 mg.; fiber - 2 gm.

ADA exchange value: 2 vegetable

POTATOES

Herbed Potato Pie

You can vary this recipe by changing the herbs you use according to what your serving for the main entree.

3 medium potatoes, thinly sliced with skins on
4 fresh basil leaves
2 Tbsp. chopped chives
2 Tbsp. fine herbs (your choice)
1 cup condensed low-sodium chicken broth

1. Preheat oven to 350°.
2. Place basil leaves in a 9-inch pie plate or quiche pan sprayed with nonstick spray. Arrange 2 layers of potatoes around the dish and sprinkle with herbs.
3. Layer the remaining potatoes on the top and pour the chicken broth over them.
4. Bake covered for 40 minutes. Remove the cover and bake 15 minutes longer.
5. Let stand for 10 minutes, then invert serving dish to remove pie.

Serves 4.

Nutrient information per serving:

calories - 90; protein - 3 gm.; carbohydrate - 20 gm.; fat - 0 gm.; saturated fat - 0 gm.; percentage of calories from fat - 1; sodium - 68 mg.; cholesterol - 0 mg.; fiber - 1 gm.

ADA exchange value: 1 starch/bread

Window-Pane Potato Chips

1 1/4 lb. baking potatoes, scrubbed and sliced very thin
1 cup assorted fresh herbs, washed and patted dry (basil, tarragon, dill, etc.)

1. Preheat oven to 450°.
2. Spray cookie sheets or jelly roll pans with olive oil. Place a layer of potato slices on sheet. Top with herb blend, then top with another layer of potato slices. Spray all slices with a light coating of olive oil.
3. Bake in batches, 7 to 10 minutes, until golden brown. (May be cooked ahead and reheated.)

Serves 6.

Nutrient information per serving:

calories - 38; protein - 1 gm.; carbohydrate - 9 gm.; fat - 0 gm.; saturated fat - 0 gm.; percentage of calories from fat - 0; sodium - 4 mg.; cholesterol - 0 mg.; fiber - 0 gm.

ADA exchange value: 1/2 starch/bread

Oven "French Fries"

Here's a healthy way to still enjoy those forbidden French Fries. Try varying this recipe by adding 1/2 tsp. of any one of the blends listed at the front of this book. You can have a crispy potato stick to accompany any international cuisine you wish.

3 large all purpose potatoes (like Russets) or about 1 1/2 lbs.
2 tsp. olive oil
1/2 tsp. salt
1/4 tsp. paprika
Freshly ground black pepper to taste

1. Set oven rack to upper level and preheat oven to 450°. Coat a baking sheet with nonstick spray. Cut each potato lengthwise into 8 wedges.
2. In large bowl combine olive oil, salt, paprika, and pepper. Add potato wedges and toss to coat.
3. Spread the potatoes on a baking sheet and roast about 20 minutes. Loosen and turn the potatoes.
4. Roast 10 to 15 minutes longer or until golden brown.

Serves 4.

Nutrient information per serving:

calories - 129; protein - 2 gm.; carbohydrate - 25 gm.; fat - 2 gm.; saturated fat - 0 gm.; percentage of calories from fat - 14; sodium - 272 mg.; cholesterol - 0 mg.; fiber - 0 gm.

ADA exchange value: 1/2 starch/bread

Mashed Potatoes

Nothing is better than homemade mashed potatoes. Here is all the flavor with none of the fat.

6 medium potatoes, washed and cubed
1 Tbsp. Butter Buds®
1/4 tsp. ground white pepper
1/2 tsp. ground nutmeg
3/4 cup skim milk

1. Place potatoes in a large Dutch oven or saucepan and cover with water. Bring to a boil and simmer until potatoes are tender.
2. Drain all the water, and mash potatoes with a masher or put potatoes through a ricer.
3. Add the remaining ingredients and whip until smooth.
4. Serve warm.

Serves 6.

Nutrient information per serving:

calories - 231; protein - 6 gm.; carbohydrate - 52 gm.; fat - 0 gm.; saturated fat - 0 gm.; percentage of calories from fat - 0; sodium - 32 mg.; cholesterol - 0 mg.; fiber - 4 gm.

ADA exchange value: 1 1/2 starch/bread

RICE AND ORZO

Indian Raisin Rice

This is a good side dish for anything that has an Indian-style flavor. It can be made with ease if you own a rice cooker.

3 1/2 cups low-salt chicken broth
1 1/2 cup brown rice
1 tsp. ground turmeric
1/2 tsp. ground cumin
1/4 tsp. ground ginger
1/8 tsp. cayenne pepper
1 cup raisins

Place all ingredients in saucepan. Bring to a boil, cover, and simmer until all liquid is absorbed (about 45 minutes).

Serves 6.

Nutrient information per serving:

calories - 150; protein - 4 gm.; carbohydrate - 25 gm.; fat - 0 gm.; saturated fat - 0 gm.; percentage of calories from fat - 2; sodium - 278 mg.; cholesterol - 0 mg.; fiber - 2 gm.

ADA exchange value: 1 starch/bread, 1/2 fruit

Lemon Rice

A perfect side dish for chicken or fish, this is especially good when cooked in a rice cooker.

2 1/2 cups low-salt chicken broth
1 cup uncooked brown rice
1 Tbsp. fresh lemon rind (2 tsp. dried)
2 Tbsp. fresh dill (2 tsp. dried)

Put broth, lemon, and dill in a saucepan and bring to a boil. Cover and simmer until liquid is absorbed.

Serves 4.

Nutrient information per serving:

calories - 61; protein - 3 gm.; carbohydrate - 11 gm.; fat - 0 gm.; saturated fat - 0 gm.; percentage of calories from fat - 6; sodium - 147 mg.; cholesterol - 0 mg.; fiber - 1 gm.

ADA exchange value: 3/4 starch/bread

Brown-Rice Pilaf

You can cook this in a rice cooker, also.

1 cup brown rice
2 cups low-sodium chicken broth
8 oz. sliced mushrooms
1 cup coarsely grated carrot
1/2 tsp. marjoram
1/4 tsp. celery seed
1/4 cup thinly sliced green onion
2 Tbsp. freshly chopped parsley

1. Bring chicken broth to boil; add all ingredients, except parsley. Bring to a boil again, then reduce to simmer. Cover and cook until all liquid is absorbed (about 45 minutes).
2. Remove from heat, add parsley, and serve.

Serves 4.

Nutrient information per serving:

calories - 86; protein - 4 gm.; carbohydrate - 17 gm.; fat - 1 gm.; saturated fat - 0 gm.; percentage of calories from fat - 0; sodium - 126 mg.; cholesterol - 0 mg.; fiber - 3 gm.

ADA exchange value: 1 starch/bread

Greek Orzo

Orzo is a pasta that looks like rice. Try it, you'll like it. And it makes a nice change from the ordinary.

2 cups orzo
1 cup water
1/2 oz. sun-dried tomatoes (packed dry)
2 oz. crumbled feta cheese
1/2 red onion, chopped
1/2 red bell pepper, chopped
1/2 green bell pepper, chopped
1/2 yellow bell pepper, chopped
2 oz. ripe olives, sliced
2 Tbsp. freshly chopped parsley
1 tsp. Greek herb blend (page 43)
4 Tbsp. wine vinegar

1. Cook orzo in water until tender. Set aside.
2. Bring 1 cup water to boil in a small sauce pan. Add sun-dried tomatoes and cook for 2 minutes. Rinse under cold water and chop.
3. Combine all ingredients in large bowl and toss.

Serves 8.

Nutrient information per serving:

calories - 99; protein - 3 gm.; carbohydrate - 14 gm.; fat - 3 gm.; saturated fat - 2 gm.; percentage of calories from fat - 29; sodium - 138 mg.; cholesterol - 8 mg.; fiber - 1 gm.

ADA exchange value: 1 starch/bread, 1/2 fat

Fried Rice

1 Tbsp. margarine
2 green onions, chopped, including tops
1 cup corn kernels
1 tsp. vegetable herb blend (page 44)
2 cups cooked brown rice
2 egg whites

1. Heat margarine in a skillet. Add onions and cook until soft.
2. Add corn, vegetable blend, and rice. Stir until warm.
3. Add egg whites, stirring until they are cooked and rice is hot.

Serves 4.

Nutrient information per serving:

calories - 315 gm.; protein - 7; carbohydrate - 63 gm.; fat - 3 gm.; saturated fat - 1 gm.; percentage of calories from fat - 10; sodium - 197 mg.; cholesterol - 0 mg.; fiber - 3 gm.

ADA exchange value: 4 starch/bread, 1/2 fat

Orzo Parmesan And Basil

1 1/2 cups orzo
3 cups low-salt chicken broth
1/3 cup freshly grated Parmesan cheese
5 Tbsp. fresh basil, chopped (or 1 1/2 tsp. dried)
Freshly ground black pepper to taste

1. Place orzo and chicken broth in a saucepan and bring to a boil. Cover and simmer until liquid is absorbed (about 20 minutes).
2. Add Parmesan cheese, basil, and pepper. Mix well.

Serves 6.

Nutrient information per serving:

calories - 70 protein - 4 gm.; carbohydrate - 9 gm.; fat - 2 gm.; saturated fat - 1 gm.; percentage of calories from fat - 22; sodium - 211 mg.; cholesterol - 4 mg.; fiber - 0 gm.

ADA exchange value: 1/2 starch/bread, 1/2 medium-fat meat

BREADS

Cinnamon Nut Bread

This is a quick and easy way to make great tasting breakfast bread that is sure to please your family and weekend guests.

11-oz. French loaf (in a can from Pillsbury Poppin Fresh®)
1/2 cup walnuts
1/4 cup brown sugar
1 tsp. ground cinnamon

1. Preheat oven to 350°.
2. Cut French bread dough in half, then cut into 20 pieces.
3. Place half the bread pieces in a ring pan sprayed well with nonstick spray
4. Place walnuts, brown sugar, and cinnamon in a mini-food chopper and grind until all is finely chopped and mixed together.
5. Sprinkle the top of the bread pieces with the nut mixture and top with remaining bread pieces.
6. Spray lightly with olive oil.
7. Bake for 30 minutes. When slightly cooled, turn bread out onto platter. Pull pieces apart for a tasty treat.

Serves 6.

Nutrient information per serving:

calories - 190; protein - 8 gm.; carbohydrate - 27 gm.; fat - 6 gm.; saturated fat - 0 gm.; percentage of calories from fat - 28; sodium - 297 mg.; cholesterol - 0 mg.; fiber - 1 gm.

ADA exchange value: 2 starch/bread

Apricot Nut Bread

A good bread for afternoon tea.

2 egg whites
2 cups low-fat buttermilk
1 tsp. vanilla
3 cups sifted all purpose flour
1 cup oat bran
1/2 cup sugar
3/4 cup dried apricots, chopped
1/4 tsp. salt
1/2 tsp. allspice
4 tsp. baking powder
1/2 cup chopped walnuts

1. Preheat oven to 325°.
2. Beat egg whites, buttermilk, and vanilla together. Set aside.
3. Combine dry ingredients. Mix in egg-and-milk mixture and chopped walnuts.
4. Pour mixture into large loaf pan sprayed with nonstick spray. Bake 45 minutes to 1 hour.
5. Turn onto wire rack and let cool before serving.

Serves 12.

Nutrient information per serving:

calories - 221; protein - 7 gm.; carbohydrate - 39 gm.; fat - 4 gm.; saturated fat - 0 gm.; percentage of calories from fat - 17; sodium - 208 mg.; cholesterol - 15 mg.; fiber - 2 gm.

ADA exchange value: 2 starch/bread, 1 fruit, 1 fat

Herbed Spoon Bread

2 1/2 cups non-fat milk
1 cup yellow cornmeal
6 egg whites, or 6 oz. egg substitute
2 Tbsp. sugar
1 tsp. baking powder
2 Tbsp. Butter Buds®
1 tsp. vegetable herb blend (page 44)
1/2 tsp. salt

1. Heat 2 cups of milk to simmer. Stir in cornmeal. When mixture becomes very thick, turn off heat.
2. Combine the remaining ingredients, including the 1/2 cup milk, mixing well.
3. Beat the two mixtures together and pour into a 2-quart baking dish sprayed with a nonstick spray.
4. Bake in preheated oven at 400° for 45 minutes.
5. Serve at once by spooning out in pieces.

Serves 6.

Nutrient information per serving:

calories - 159; protein - 9 gm.; carbohydrate - 29 gm.; fat - 0 gm.; saturated fat - 0 gm.; percentage of calories from fat - 3; sodium - 418 mg.; cholesterol - 2 mg.; fiber - 1 gm.

ADA exchange value: 2 starch/bread, 1 lean meat

Pumpkin Muffins

1 1/2 cups unbleached flour
1/2 cup brown sugar
1/4 cup molasses
2 tsp. cinnamon
1/4 tsp. allspice
1/4 tsp. ginger
1/4 tsp. ground cloves
1 cup canned solid pumpkin
1/2 cup skim milk
4 oz. egg substitute
1/2 cup chopped dates
1/2 cup chopped walnuts

1. Mix all dry ingredients together. Set aside.
2. Combine all liquid ingredients. Add dry ingredients and mix until moistened.
3. Fold in dates and nuts.
4. Spoon into 24 muffin tins sprayed with nonstick spray.
5. Bake for 15 minutes in preheated oven at 375° or until done.

Serves 24.

Nutrient information per serving:

calories - 82; protein - 2 gm.; carbohydrate - 15 gm.; fat - 2 gm.; saturated fat - 0 gm.; percentage of calories from fat - 18; sodium - 50 mg.; cholesterol - 0 mg.; fiber - 1 gm.

ADA exchange value: 1 starch/bread

Cheddar Beer Bread

3 cups unbleached flour
1 Tbsp. baking powder
1 tsp. herb salt blend (page 42)
1 Tbsp. sugar
1 cup grated sharp cheddar cheese
1 cup grated mozzarella cheese
1/2 cup diced onion
12 oz. can beer

1. Preheat oven to 350°.
2. Combine all ingredients except beer and mix well.
3. Slowly add beer until all is well blended.
4. Spoon mixture into loaf pan sprayed with nonstick spray.
5. Smooth down mixture until even. Bake 1 hour.

Serves 8.

Nutrient information per serving:

calories - 233; protein - 8 gm.; carbohydrate - 37 gm.; fat - 4 gm.; saturated fat - 2 gm.; percentage of calories from fat - 15; sodium - 297 mg.; cholesterol - 11 mg.; fiber - 1 gm.

ADA exchange value: 2 starch/bread, 1 medium fat meat

Nut Bread

This is a perfect bread to serve with a large salad at a luncheon or as a light supper. You can either bake this in one large loaf pan or split it into two smaller loaves so you can freeze one of them for use later.

2 egg whites
2 cups non-fat milk
1 Tbsp. Butter Buds®
1 tsp. vanilla
3 cups sifted all-purpose flour
1 cup rolled oats
3/4 cup sugar
1/4 tsp. salt
1 tsp. allspice
1/4 tsp. cinnamon
4 tsp. baking powder
1/2 cup chopped walnuts

1. Preheat oven to 325°.
2. Beat egg whites, milk, Butter Buds, and vanilla together. Set aside.
3. Combine dry ingredients. Mix in milk mixture and chopped walnuts.
4. Pour into large loaf pan sprayed with nonstick spray. Bake for 45 minutes to 1 hour.
5. Turn onto a wire rack and let cool before serving.

Serves 12.

Nutrient information per serving:

calories - 228; protein - 7 gm.; carbohydrate - 41 gm.; fat - 4 gm.; saturated fat - 0 gm.; percentage of calories from fat - 15; sodium - 208 mg.; cholesterol - 1 mg.; fiber - 1 gm.

ADA exchange value: 2 1/2 starch/bread, 1/2 fat

Ginger Banana Bread

Coffee is another spice that has some healthful properties. Here I've used it in a delicious banana bread recipe. Another secret ingredient that adds to the flavor is the touch of ginger. Hope you like it!

2/3 cup packed brown sugar
1/3 cup hot, strong, brewed coffee
1 1/2 cups mashed overripe bananas (about 4 whole bananas)
1 large egg
1 large egg white
3 Tbsp. vegetable oil plus a little to oil the pan
1 tsp. pure vanilla extract
1 cup all purpose white flour
1 cup whole wheat flour
1 1/2 tsp. baking powder
1 tsp. cinnamon
1 tsp. ground ginger
1/2 tsp. salt
1/4 tsp. baking soda

1. Preheat the oven to 350°. Lightly oil a 9 x 5-inch loaf pan.
2. In a medium bowl, dissolve brown sugar in coffee and stir in bananas.
3. In a large bowl, whisk together egg, egg white, oil, and vanilla. Add banana mixture.
4. In another separate bowl, whisk together flours, baking powder, cinnamon, ginger, salt, and baking soda. Add to banana mixture and stir just until combined.
5. Pour mixture into loaf pan. Bake 40 to 50 minutes or until toothpick comes out clean.

Serves 12.

Nutrient information per serving:

calories - 163; protein - 46 gm.; carbohydrate - 37 gm.; fat - 4 gm.; saturated fat - 1 gm.; percentage of calories from fat - 22; sodium - 163 mg.; cholesterol - 18 mg.; fiber - 0 gm.

ADA exchange value: 1 starch/bread

Cheese Monkey Bread

This is a quick and easy way to make great tasting bread that will highlight any dish.

11-oz. French loaf (in can from Pillsbury Poppin Fresh®)
1/2 cup low-fat cheddar cheese, grated
2 tsp. paprika
1/4 tsp. cayenne pepper

1. Preheat oven to 350°.
2. Cut French bread dough in half then into 20 pieces.
3. Place half the bread pieces in a loaf pan sprayed with nonstick spray,
4. Sprinkle the top with cheese, paprika, and cayenne pepper. Top with remaining bread pieces.
5. Spray lightly with olive oil spray. Bake for 30 minutes. When slightly cooled, turn bread onto a platter. Pull apart to serve.

Serves 6.

Nutrient information per serving:

calories - 132; protein - 11 gm.; carbohydrate - 16 gm.; fat - 2 gm.; saturated fat - 0 gm.; percentage of calories from fat - 14; sodium - 393 mg.; cholesterol - 7 mg.; fiber - 0 gm.

ADA exchange value: 1 starch/bread, 1/2 lean meat

Cornbread With Green Chilies

1 cup hot water
1/4 cup sun-dried tomatoes (packed dry)
1 cup all-purpose flour
1 cup yellow cornmeal
2 Tbsp. sugar
1 tsp. baking powder
1/2 tsp. herb salt blend (page 42)
1/2 tsp. marjoram
1 cup low-fat buttermilk
8 oz. egg substitute
1 cup corn kernels
1/2 cup green onion, sliced thin
4-oz. can green chilies

1. Preheat oven to 375°.
2. Place tomatoes in hot water and let stand 10 minutes, then chop.
3. Combine all dry ingredients in a large bowl.
4. Combine all liquid ingredients, mixing well.
5. Stir liquid into dry mixture, then add corn, onions, and chilies. Stir in well.
6. Pour mixture into a 9-inch square baking pan coated with non-stick spray.
7. Bake for 30 minutes or until done.

Serves 12.

Nutrient information per serving:

calories - 117; protein - 5 gm.; carbohydrate - 23 gm.; fat - 0 gm.; saturated fat - 0 gm.; percentage of calories from fat - 0; sodium - 307 mg.; cholesterol - 0 mg.; fiber - 2 gm.

ADA exchange value: 1 1/2 starch/bread

Poppy Seed Rolls

This is a quick and lazy way to make dinner rolls. You can use caraway seeds or sesame seeds instead of poppy seed to vary this recipe.

1-11-oz. French bread (in a can from Pillsbury Poppin Fresh®)
2 Tbsp. poppy seeds

1. Preheat oven to 350°.
2. Cut bread into 12 pieces. Roll each piece in poppy seeds.
3. Spray a cookie sheet with nonstick spray or line it with foil. (I like using the foil because clean-up is so easy.)
4. Place rolls on cookie sheet and spray lightly with olive oil.
5. Bake until brown (about 10 to 12 minutes).

Serves 6.

Nutrient information per serving:

calories - 92; protein - 5 gm.; carbohydrate - 16 gm.; fat - 0 gm.; saturated fat - 0 gm. percentage of calories from fat - 0; sodium - 293 mg.; cholesterol - 0 mg.; fiber - 0 gm.

ADA exchange value: 1 starch/bread

Easy Herbed Dinner Rolls

2 1/4 cups all-purpose flour
2 Tbsp. sugar
1 tsp. salt
1 tsp. caraway seed
1 Tbsp. snipped fresh sage leaves (or 1/2 tsp. dried sage leaves), crumbled
1/4 tsp. ground nutmeg
1 package active dry yeast
1 cup very warm water
2 Tbsp. shortening
1 egg

1. Combine 1 1/4 cups flour, sugar, salt, caraway seed, sage, nutmeg, and yeast in large bowl. Add water, shortening, and egg; beat until smooth. Stir in remaining flour until smooth. Scrape batter from sides of bowl. Cover and let rise in warm place until doubled, about 30 minutes.
2. Spray 12 medium muffin cups (2 1/2 by 1 1/4 inches) with nonstick spray.
3. Stir batter, beating about 25 strokes. Spoon into muffin cups. Let rise a second time until batter rounds over tops of cups, about 20 minutes.
4. Heat oven to 400°. Bake rolls until golden brown, about 15 minutes. Serve warm.

Makes one dozen rolls.

Nutrient information per serving:

calories - 115; protein - 3 gm.; carbohydrate - 19 gm.; fat - 3 gm.; saturated fat - 0 gm.; percentage of calories from fat - 23; sodium - 190 mg.; cholesterol - 25 mg.; fiber - 0 gm.

ADA exchange value: 1 starch/bread

DESSERTS

Peach Bread Pudding

This is a nice twist on the traditional bread pudding. You can serve it with nonfat ice cream or frozen nonfat yogurt. Or you can top it with light whipped topping.

1 12-oz. can condensed skim milk
1 1/2 cup skim milk
8 oz. egg substitute
1/2 cup sugar
1/2 tsp. nutmeg
1 tsp. cinnamon
1 lb. white bread, crust removed
16-oz. pkg. frozen peaches without sugar, thawed

1. Preheat oven to 350°. Spray a 9-inch x 13-inch baking pan with a nonstick spray.
2. Mix milk, egg substitute, sugar, nutmeg, and cinnamon.
3. Put a layer of bread on the bottom of the baking pan. Pour half the liquid over the bread.
4. Spread the peaches evenly over the bread. Top with remaining bread.
5. Pour remaining milk mixture over the top.
6. Bake 60 minutes. Serve warm or cold.

Serves 8.

Nutrient information per serving:

calories - 266; protein - 12 gm.; carbohydrate - 50 gm.; fat - 2 gm.; saturated fat - 0 gm.; percentage of calories from fat - 6; sodium - 378 mg.; cholesterol - 4 mg.; fiber - 2 gm.

ADA exchange value: 2 starch/bread, 1 1/2 fruit

Pumpkin Cake

The perfect holiday gift, this recipe will make two large Bundt® cakes or four small ones.

Mix together:

8 oz. egg substitute
1 cup brown sugar
1/2 cup sugar
1 tsp. vanilla
1 cup skim milk
1 28-oz. can solid pumpkin

Mix together:

2 cups all-purpose flour
2 cups oatmeal
1 Tbsp. baking soda
1 tsp. baking powder
3 Tbsp. pumpkin pie spice
2 cups chopped walnuts
1 cup raisins

1. Fold dry ingredients into liquid until well mixed.
2. Pour mixture into 2 large or 4 small Bundt® pans sprayed with non-stick spray.
3. Bake in preheated oven at 350°, 45 minutes for 4 small cakes or 60 minutes for 2 large cakes.
4. Let cool. Unmold on plates and sprinkle with powdered sugar before serving.

Each recipe makes 24 servings.

Nutrient information per serving:

calories - 218; protein - 7 gm.; carbohydrate - 35 gm.; fat - 7 gm.; saturated fat - 0 gm.; percentage of calories from fat - 26; sodium - 190 mg.; cholesterol - 0 mg.; fiber - 2 gm.

ADA exchange value: 2 starch/bread, 1 lean meat, 1 fat

Orange Sponge Cake

1 cup cake flour
1 tsp. baking powder
1/4 tsp. salt
2 oz. egg substitute (make sure you use one with 0 grams fat)
3/4 cup sugar
2 tsp. pure vanilla extract
1 tsp. allspice
1 tsp. cinnamon
1/2 tsp. nutmeg
1/4 cup water
1 Tbsp. orange rind
1/4 cup concentrated orange juice
5 egg whites

1. Sift flour, baking powder, and salt together. Set aside.
2. Beat egg substitute with 1/2 cup sugar, vanilla, allspice, cinnamon, nutmeg, and water.
3. Add flour mixture to egg mixture and mix well.
4. In a separate bowl, beat egg whites, gradually adding remaining 1/4 cup sugar until stiff peaks form.
5. Fold egg whites into flour mixture.
6. Spray a 10-inch tube pan with a nonstick spray. Pour cake batter into pan and bake in a preheated oven at 350° for 35 minutes.
7. Let cool 45 minutes before serving.

Serves 8.

Nutrient information per serving:

calories - 152; protein - 4 gm.; carbohydrate - 33 gm.; fat - 0 gm.; saturated fat - 0 gm.; percentage of calories from fat - 1; sodium - 158 mg.; cholesterol - 0 mg.; fiber - 0 gm.

ADA exchange value: 1 starch/bread, 1 fruit

Chocolate-Chip Sponge Cake

1 cup cake flour
1 tsp. baking powder
1/4 tsp. salt
4 oz. egg substitute (make sure you use the one with 0 fat grams)
3/4 cup sugar
2 tsp. pure vanilla extract
1 tsp. almond extract
1/4 cup water
5 egg whites
1/2 cup mini semisweet chocolate chips

1. Sift flour, baking powder, and salt together. Set aside.
2. Beat egg substitute with 1/2 cup sugar, vanilla, almond extract, and water.
3. Add flour mixture to egg mixture and mix well.
4. In a separate bowl, beat egg whites, gradually adding remaining 1/4 cup sugar until stiff peaks form.
5. Fold egg whites and chocolate chips into flour mixture.
6. Spray a 10-inch tube pan with nonstick spray. Pour cake batter into pan and bake in preheated oven at 350° for 35 minutes.
7. Let cool 45 minutes before serving.

Serves 8.

Nutrient information per serving:

calories - 200; protein - 6 gm.; carbohydrate - 36 gm.; fat - 4 gm.; saturated fat - 2 gm.; percentage of calories from fat - 17; sodium - 182 mg.; cholesterol - 0 mg.; fiber - 1 gm.

ADA exchange value: 2 starch/bread, 1 fat

Peach Cobbler

16-oz. pkg. frozen sliced peaches, no sugar added, thawed
1 cup peach nectar
1/2 tsp. cinnamon
1/4 tsp. nutmeg
2 Tbsp. cornstarch
2 cups (3 oz.) low-fat granola cereal

1. Place peaches in a souffle dish that has been sprayed with non-stick spray.
2. Combine nectar, cinnamon, nutmeg, and cornstarch and stir well.
3. Pour liquid over peaches and mix.
4. Cover the top with granola and bake in a preheated oven at 350° for 30 minutes.
5. Let cool at least 10 minutes before serving.

Serves 4.

Nutrient information per serving:

calories - 175; protein - 3 gm.; carbohydrate - 41 gm.; fat - 2 gm.; saturated fat - 0 gm.; percentage of calories from fat - 8; sodium - 49 mg.; cholesterol - 0 mg.; fiber - 3 gm.

ADA exchange value: 1 1/2 starch/bread, 1 fruit

Chocolate Spice Bars

3 egg whites
1/3 cup skim milk
1 tsp. vanilla
2/3 cup sugar
1/2 tsp. mace
2 tsp. instant coffee, mixed in 1/4 cup hot water
1 cup solid canned pumpkin
1 cup unbleached flour
1 cup self-rising flour
1/4 cup imported cocoa powder
3/4 cup mini semisweet chocolate chips

1. Mix together egg whites, skim milk, vanilla, sugar, mace, coffee, and pumpkin.
2. Sift flour and cocoa powder into liquid mixture and mix well.
3. Fold in chocolate chips.
4. Pour into a tube pan sprayed with nonstick spray.
5. Bake in a preheated oven at 350° for 35 minutes.
6. Cool and cut into 20 bars.

Serves 20.

Nutrient information per serving:

calories - 115; protein - 3 gm.; carbohydrate - 21 gm.; fat - 3 gm.; saturated fat - 1 gm.; percentage of calories from fat - 20; sodium - 12 mg.; cholesterol - 0 mg.; fiber - 1 gm.

ADA exchange value: 1 starch/bread, 1/2 fruit, 1/2 fat

Brownies

Yes, you can still enjoy brownies. If you can balance a little extra fat in your diet, add 1/2 cup walnuts folded in with the chocolate chips, or sprinkle them on top before baking.

4 egg whites
1/2 cup skim milk
1 tsp. vanilla
2/3 cup sugar
1 cup solid canned pumpkin
1 cup unbleached flour
1 cup self-rising flour
1/2 cup imported cocoa powder
3/4 cup mini semi-sweet chocolate chips

1. Mix together egg whites, non-fat milk, vanilla, sugar, and pumpkin.
2. Sift flour and cocoa powder into liquid mixture and mix well.
3. Fold in chocolate chips.
4. Pour into a tube pan sprayed with nonstick spray.
5. Bake in preheated oven at 350° for 35 minutes.
6. Cool and cut into 20 bars.

Serves 20.

Nutrient information per serving:

calories - 115; protein - 3 gm.; carbohydrate - 21 gm.; fat - 3 gm.; saturated fat - 1 gm.; percentage of calories from fat - 20; sodium - 12 mg.; cholesterol - 0 mg.; fiber - 1 gm.

ADA exchange value: 1 starch/bread, 1/2 fruit, 1/2 fat

Spiced Apricots

These can be served hot or cold and are delicious with chicken, ham, or pork.

28-oz. can apricot halves in light syrup, drained reserving 1 cup liquid
2 Tbsp. cornstarch
2 Tbsp. brown sugar
1 tsp. pumpkin pie spice
1 Tbsp. white wine vinegar

1. Combine cornstarch, sugar, pumpkin pie spice, and vinegar in a saucepan and bring to a boil.
2. Lower heat and add apricots. Simmer 10 minutes.

Serves 6.

Nutrient information per serving:

calories - 147; protein - 1 gm.; carbohydrate - 38 gm.; fat - 0 gm.; saturated fat - 0 gm.; percentage of calories from fat - 1; sodium - 7 mg.; cholesterol - 0 mg.; fiber - 2 gm.

ADA exchange value: 2 fruit

Basic Sponge Cake

This is an all-around cake recipe you can use as the basis for a multitude of cake creations—all with no fat!

1 cup cake flour
1 tsp. baking powder
1/4 tsp. salt
4 oz. egg substitute (make sure you use the one with 0 grams fat)
3/4 cup sugar
2 tsp. pure vanilla extract
1 tsp. almond extract
1/4 cup water
5 egg whites

1. Sift flour, baking powder, and salt together. Set aside.
2. Beat egg substitute with 1/2 cup sugar, vanilla, and water.
3. Add flour mixture to egg mixture and mix well.
4. In a separate bowl, beat egg whites, gradually adding remaining 1/4 cup sugar until stiff peaks form.
5. Fold egg whites into flour mixture.
6. Spray a 10-inch tube pan with a nonstick spray, pour cake batter into pan, and bake in a preheated oven at 350° for 35 minutes.
7. Let cool 45 minutes before serving.

Serves 8.

Nutrient information per serving:

calories - 146; protein - 5 gm.; carbohydrate - 30 gm.; fat - 0 gm.; saturated fat - 0 gm.; percentage of calories from fat - 0; sodium - 182 mg.; cholesterol - 0 mg.; fiber - 0 gm.

ADA exchange value: 2 starch/bread

Almond Tofu Cake

This is a great cake to use for snacks throughout the day. Just cut and wrap the pieces. It's also a wonderful cake to use for strawberry or peach shortcake.

14 oz. soft tofu
1/2 cup almonds
1/2 cup sugar
1 tsp. vanilla
2 tsp. almond extract
6 egg whites
1 1/2 tsp. baking powder
2 1/2 cups all-purpose flour

1. Put all ingredients, except egg whites, baking powder, and flour, in a food processor with a steel blade and process well.
2. Sift baking powder and flour into a large bowl. Fold in tofu mixture.
3. Beat egg whites to soft peaks and fold into mixture.
4. Pour into a round 10-inch baking pan sprayed with nonstick spray.
5. Bake in preheated oven at 350° for 25 minutes.

Serves 10.

Nutrient information per serving:

calories - 221; protein - 9 gm.; carbohydrate - 34 gm.; fat - 5 gm.; saturated fat - 1 gm.; percentage of calories from fat - 19; sodium - 93 mg.; cholesterol - 0 mg.; fiber - 1 gm.

ADA exchange value: 2 starch/bread, 1 medium fat meat

Lemon Sponge Cake

This is a variation of the basic sponge cake recipe that shows just one of the ways you be creative using this recipe. The best part is, of course, there is no fat!

1 cup cake flour
1 tsp. baking powder
1/4 tsp. salt
2 oz. egg substitute (remember, use one with 0 grams of fat)
3/4 cup sugar
2 tsp. pure vanilla extract
1/4 cup pure lemon juice
1 Tbsp. lemon rind
5 egg whites

1. Sift flour, baking powder, and salt together. Set aside.
2. Beat egg substitute with 1/2 cup sugar, vanilla, lemon juice, and rind.
3. Add flour mixture to egg mixture and mix well.
4. In a separate bowl, beat egg whites, gradually adding remaining 1/4 cup sugar until stiff peaks form.
5. Fold egg whites into flour mixture.
6. Spray a 10-inch tube pan with nonstick spray. Pour cake batter into pan and bake in preheated oven at 350° for 35 minutes.
7. Let cool 45 minutes before serving.

Serves 8.

Nutrient information per serving:

calories - 140; protein - 4 gm.; carbohydrate - 30 gm.; fat - 0 gm.; saturated fat - 0 gm.; percentage of calories from fat - 0; sodium - 159 mg.; cholesterol - 0 mg.; fiber - 0 gm.

ADA exchange value: 2 starch/bread

Poppy-Seed Sponge Cake

Here's that basic recipe again, this time dressed up with poppy seeds for an exciting alternate flavor.

1 cup cake flour
1 tsp. baking powder
1/4 tsp. salt
2 oz. egg substitute (with 0 grams of fat)
3/4 cup sugar
2 tsp. pure vanilla extract
2 Tbsp. poppy seeds
1/4 cup water
5 egg whites

1. Sift flour, baking powder, and salt together. Set aside.
2. Beat egg substitute with 1/2 cup sugar, vanilla, poppy seeds, and water.
3. Add flour mixture to egg mixture and mix well.
4. In a separate bowl, beat egg whites, gradually adding remaining 1/4 cup sugar until stiff peaks form.
5. Fold egg whites into flour mixture.
6. Spray a 10-inch tube pan with nonstick spray, pour cake batter into pan, and bake in preheated oven at 350° for 35 minutes.
7. Let cool 45 minutes before serving.

Serves 8.

Nutrient information per serving:

calories - 158; protein - 4 gm.; carbohydrate - 30 gm.; fat - 0 gm.; saturated fat - 0 gm.; percentage of calories from fat - 0; sodium - 157 mg.; cholesterol - 0 mg.; fiber - 0 gm.

ADA exchange value: 2 starch/bread,

Spice Sponge Cake

Another variation of that delicious sponge cake.

1 cup cake flour
1 tsp. baking powder
1/4 tsp. salt
2 oz. egg substitute (with no fat)
3/4 cup sugar
2 tsp. pure vanilla extract
1 tsp. allspice
1 tsp. cinnamon
1/2 tsp. nutmeg
1/4 cup water
5 egg whites

1. Sift flour, baking powder, and salt together. Set aside.
2. Beat egg substitute with 1/2 cup sugar, vanilla, allspice, cinnamon, nutmeg, and water.
3. Add flour mixture to egg mixture and mix well.
4. In a separate bowl, beat egg whites, gradually adding remaining 1/4 cup sugar until stiff peaks form.
5. Fold egg whites into flour mixture.
6. Spray a 10-inch tube pan with nonstick spray. Pour cake batter into pan and bake in a preheated oven at 350° for 35 minutes.
7. Let cool 45 minutes before serving.

Serves 8.

Nutrient information per serving:

calories - 138; protein - 47 gm.; carbohydrate - 30 gm.; fat - 0 gm.; saturated fat - 0 gm.; percentage of calories from fat - 0; sodium - 157 mg.; cholesterol - 0 mg.; fiber - 0 gm.

ADA exchange value: 2 starch/bread

Tomato Soup Cake

This was a family favorite at our house. It still is, but now it is more healthful.

2 cups sifted flour
2 tsp. baking powder
1 tsp. cinnamon
1 tsp. nutmeg
1/2 tsp. ground cloves
4 oz. egg substitute
3/4 cup sugar
1 10 3/4-oz. can tomato soup
1/2 cup chopped walnuts

1. Preheat oven to 350°.
2. Sift flour, baking powder, cinnamon, nutmeg, and cloves together and set aside.
3. Combine egg substitute, sugar, and tomato soup. Gradually add flour mixture into liquid mixture.
4. Stir in walnuts.
5. Pour into a Bundt® pan that has been sprayed with nonstick spray.
6. Bake for 25 to 30 minutes (check for doneness with a wooden toothpick).

Serves 8.

Nutrient information per serving:

calories - 258; protein - 7 gm.; carbohydrate - 47 gm.; fat - 5 gm.; saturated fat - 0 gm. percentage of calories from fat - 17; sodium - 391 mg.; cholesterol - 0 mg.; fiber - 1 gm.

ADA exchange value: 3 starch/bread, 1 fat

INDEX